Intellectual Property Law

in

Cyberspace

Second Edition

2012 Supplement

Intellectual Property Titles from Bloomberg BNA

Anatomy of a Patent Case by American College of Trial Lawyers

Biotechnology and the Federal Circuit by Kenneth J. Burchfiel

Constructing and Deconstructing Patents by Irah H. Donner

Copyright Law Deskbook by Robert W. Clarida

Drafting Patent License Agreements by Brian G. Brunsvold, D. Patrick O'Reilley, and D. Brian Kacedon

Drafting Patents for Litigation and Licensing Bradley C. Wright, *Editor-in-Chief*

Electronic and Software Patents: Law and Practice Steven W. Lundberg, Stephen C. Durant, and Ann M. McCrackin, *Editors-in-Chief* and AIPLA

Harmon on Patents: Black-Letter Law and Commentary by Robert L. Harmon

Intellectual Property Law in Cyberspace by G. Peter Albert, Jr. and AIPLA

Intellectual Property, Software, and Information Licensing: Law and Practice by Xuan-Thao N. Nguyen, Robert W. Gomulkiewicz, and Danielle Conway

Intellectual Property Taxation: Transaction and Litigation Issues by Jeffrey A. Maine and Xuan-Thao N. Nguyen

Intellectual Property Technology Transfer Aline C. Flower, *Editor-in-Chief*

International Patent Litigation: A Country-by-Country Analysis Edited by Michael N. Meller and William O. Hennessey

Patents and the Federal Circuit by Robert L. Harmon, Cynthia A. Homan, and Charles M. McMahon

Patent Law and Practice by Herbert F. Schwartz and Robert J. Goldman

Patent Infringement Remedies by Lawrence M. Sung

Patent Litigation Strategies Handbook Barry L. Grossman and Gary M. Hoffman, *Editors-in-Chief*

Patent Prosecution: Law, Practice, and Procedure by Irah H. Donner

Patent, Trademark, and Copyright Laws Edited by Jeffrey M. Samuels

Pharmaceutical Patent Law by John R. Thomas

Post-Grant Patent Practice by Nancy J. Linck, Bruce H. Stoner, Jr., Lee E. Barrett, and Carol A. Spiegel

Products Comparison Manual for Trademark Users by Francis M. Pinckney and David R. Higgins

Trademark Dilution: Federal, State, and International Law by David S. Welkowitz

Trademark Infringement Remedies Brian E. Banner, *Editor-in-Chief*

Trademark Litigation Practice by David S. Fleming and John T. Gabrielides

For details on these and other related titles, please visit our Web site at *bna.com/bnabooks* or call 1-800-960-1220 to request a catalog.
All books are available on a 30-day free-examination basis.

Intellectual Property Law

in

Cyberspace

Second Edition

2012 Supplement

G. Peter Albert, Jr.
and
American
Intellectual Property Law
Association

AIPLA

American
Intellectual Property Law
Association
Arlington, VA

Bloomberg
BNA

Bloomberg BNA , Arlington, VA

Library of Congress Cataloging-in-Publication Data

Albert, G. Peter, 1964–
    Intellectual property law in cyberspace / G. Peter Albert, Jr. -- 2nd ed.
        p. cm.
    Includes bibliographical references and index.
    ISBN 978-1-57018-753-7 (alk. paper)
    1.   Industrial property--United States. 2. Computer networks--Law and
legislation--United States. 3. Internet 4. Copyright and electronic data
processing--United States. I. Title.
    KF3095.A77 2011
    346.7304'8--dc23

                                                                    2011040494

Published by Bloomberg BNA
1801 S. Bell Street, Arlington, VA 22202
bna.com/bnabooks

ISBN 978-1-61746-071-5
Printed in the United States of America

Preface

I am writing this preface on the eve of Election Day 2012, one of the closest and most expensive presidential campaigns in our country's history. I naturally cannot stop thinking, "Who is in the lead now?" Trying to answer this question highlights the current relevancy of the Internet- and Internet-related practices that are discussed in this supplement, as well as in the main volume. Once I might have relied only on sample polls to get an indication of which way voters are leaning, but today I can also look at the money the candidates have spent on Internet advertising, as well as the latest social media trends.

For instance, Barack Obama apparently receives more traffic to his Web site than Mitt Romney—especially from first-time visitors. Traffic from first-timers rose by almost 5 million from April 2012 to August 2012. This high influx of visits over such a short period of time likely indicates that more people are clicking on ads for Obama's Web site. Both Obama and Romney engaged in PPC (pay per click) advertising, such as Google's Adwords program, but Obama's campaign is spending more, overall, on Adwords, even though Romney is paying more per "click." This may confirm that more people are clicking on Obama's ads than Romney's. Obama may also get more traffic to his site because he has better "search engine optimization," or SEO. Apparently, Obama's site has significantly more "rankings" than Romney's. "Rankings" refer to top placements on search engine results pages, and are largely attributed to the number of incoming links from third party Web sites. (In this way, search engines seem to operate much like Presidential election: the candidate—or the Web site—with the most votes wins the highest rank.)

Looking at social media sources, the lead that Obama has over Romney in Facebook fans and Twitter followers is staggering (although possibly not surprising given that the majority of these social media users fall in the middle class income range.)

In 24 hours I will know if using trends in social media and Internet advertising was an inaccurate way of predicting the 2012 presidential winner. However, I am confident that social media and the Internet will continue to be a battleground for Presidential candidates looking to influence voters. And I know that the relevancy of Internet practices will only increase—whether they are used in politics, business, world affairs, popular culture, or personal habit.

It is because of relevancy of these Internet practices in the world today that the authors of Intellectual Law in Cyberspace and its annual supplements are excited to report on cyberspace developments, in the courts and on Capitol Hill. The 2012 Cumulative supplement includes discussion of:

- The *Rosetta Stone* decision, in which the Fourth Circuit reversed summary judgment rulings in Google's favor on the issue of direct trademark infringement, contributory infringement, and dilution claims, to revisit the question of whether using trademarks to trigger sponsored links can cause actual consumer confusion;

- The Ninth Circuit's ruling in *Network Automation Inc. v. Advanced Systems Concepts*, involving the sale of a trademark by search engines, most prominently GoogleAdWord and Microsoft Bing, to trigger links sponsored by a competitor, in which the court distinctly rejected the application of the "Internet trinity" or "troika" factors of *Brookfield* as the test for trademark infringement;

- A California federal district court's excellent review of case law involving the copyrightability of computer programs via a thorough analysis of application program interfaces, or APIs, in *Oracle America v. Google*;

- The steps taken by Pinterest, a social networking site, to protect itself from allegations of copyright infringement when a user creates online collections, or pinboards, of images, including copyrighted images;

- A new subsection discussing browsewrap/clickwrap hybrid developments;

- An updated survey on Internet jurisdictional and notice issues, including those involving Facebook, from a New York federal district court's decision in *Fteja v. Facebook, Inc.*, where the court enforced the forum selection clause contained in Facebook's terms of service requiring all actions to be brought in California; but, in *Fraley v. Facebook, Inc.*, a California federal district court rejected Facebook's motion to dismiss in part because it found there to be a disputed issue of fact as to whether plaintiffs had validly consented to a provision in Facebook's Statement of Rights and Responsibilities;

- A decision from the European Union's highest court in May 2012, *SAS Institute, Inc. v. World Programming Ltd.*, which reaffirmed the legality of reverse engineering on an international scale;

- Two recent bills introduced in Congress that reflect growing concerns over what should be considered permissible with respect to accessing a person's e-mail; and

- A discussion of the Obama Administration's introduction, in February 2012, of a "Framework for Protecting Privacy of Consumer Data in Digital Economy," concerned with how private-sector entities handle personal data in online commercial settings.

I am so grateful to all of the contributing authors of this 2012 supplement, and special gratitude must be extended to Jim Fattibene and Wendy Leibowitz of Bloomberg BNA for their patience and support.

G. PETER ALBERT, JR.
ALBERT DHAND LLP
SAN DIEGO, CALIFORNIA

November 2012

About the Authors

EDITOR-IN-CHIEF

G. Peter Albert, Jr. is an intellectual property and technology attorney who practiced law at large general practice and intellectual property firms in Chicago and San Diego for more than 17 years before starting his own intellectual property and technology law boutique firm, AlbertDhand LLP, in 2010. Martindale Hubble has given Peter a peer review rating of *AV Preeminent 5.0 out of 5.0* (the highest rating possible) indicating that Peter's peers rank him at the highest level of professional excellence in general ethical standards and legal ability. *The San Diego Daily Transcript* has selected him numerous times as a San Diego County Top Attorney. Peter's practice encompasses all phases of international patent, trademark, and copyright litigation, prosecution, licensing and intellectual property counseling. He is a frequent lecturer on intellectual property law and an adjunct professor of various intellectual property and technology law courses at the University of San Diego Law School and Chicago Kent School of Law. He is also the author of the legal treatise *Intellectual Property Law in Cyberspace* (BNA Books (1999) and supplements (2000, 2002, 2003–2007) and is a contributing author of the legal treatise *Legal issues in Electronic Commerce* (Captus Press, 2002 and 2005). Peter is licensed to practice law in Michigan, Illinois, and California, and is registered to practice in the U.S. Patent and Trademark Office.

G. Peter Albert, Jr.
Rita Abbati Albert

Chapters 1 and 2: Search Engines; Links and Frames

Rita Abbati Albert is an intellectual property attorney certified to practice in Illinois and California, and before the U.S. Patent and Trademark Office. For the last 10 years, she has worked in private practice and taught intellectual property issues as an adjunct professor at University of San Diego Law School, Chicago-Kent College of Law and Thomas Jefferson School of Law. She is a co-author of the original Intellectual Property

Law in Cyberspace, first published in 1999, and of its subsequent supplements (2000–2006). Ms. Albert currently works as counsel for Brighter Futures for Beautiful Minds, Inc., and is active in the nonprofit world, serving on boards and committees and as legal counsel for several nonprofits, including The Children's School, ConnectMed International and Elite Rugby Foundation.

Stephen J. Weed

Chapter 3: Web Crawlers

Stephen J. Weed is a Shareholder in the Valley Forge office of Ratner-Prestia. He received his B.S.E.E. from Iowa State University and his J.D. from Wayne State University Law School. Mr. Weed is a member of the Association of University Technology Managers (AUTM), the American Intellectual Property Law Association, the Philadelphia Intellectual Property Law Association, and the Chester County Bar Association. Additionally, he is a Registered Patent Attorney admitted to practice before the United States Patent and Trademark Office (PTO). Mr. Weed presently serves as secretary of the AIPLA Electronic and Computer Law Committee and as a board member of PIPLA; and is active on the AUTM Web site redesign committee. He has spoken at the Joint Patent Practice Seminar in New York, AUTM Annual and Regional meetings, the 2012 PIPLA Year in Review, and the 2012 AIPLA Annual Meeting. Mr. Weed entered the private practice of law in 1998 after working six years as an analyst for Electronic Data Systems (EDS). Mr. Weed's practice focuses on the procurement of IP rights, the assessment of IP rights, and the transfer of IP rights for electrical, electromechanical, mechanical, business method, and computer developments. His areas of expertise include: analog and digital circuits, medical devices, semiconductor fabrication, data encryption, telecommunications, television, financial software, and Internet technologies.

Scott W. Pink

Chapter 4: Using and Protecting Copyrighted Works on the Internet

Scott W. Pink is special counsel in the Sacramento, California office of DLA Piper. Mr. Pink concentrates in advising technology, media, entertainment and a variety of consumer product and franchise companies on intellectual property protection and litigation, advertising and promotional issues, gift cards, sweepstakes, contests and loyalty programs, trademark and copyright protection, commercial and technology transactions, e-commerce, social media and Internet law, and privacy and security issues. He serves as the lead outside advertising and marketing counsel to several well-known brands.

Mr. Pink has served as chair of local, state, and national intellectual property organizations, including the San Francisco and Sacramento Bar's Intellectual Property Sections, the California State Bar's Intellectual Property Section, the American Corporate Counsel Association's national Intellectual Property Committee and the American Bar Association's Cybersecurity Task Force. He has spoken to many organizations on the subject of marketing and promotions, intellectual property law, privacy and security, Internet law and strategic alliances. He has been recognized as a Northern California Super Lawyer by *San Francisco and Law & Politics* magazines and listed in *The Best Lawyers in America* for his intellectual property practice. Mr. Pink is currently the Pro Bono Coordinator for the firm's Sacramento office.

Joshua L. Simmons

Chapter 5: The Digital Millennium Copyright Act and Its Effect on Copyright Owners and Service Providers Online

Joshua Simmons is an attorney in the New York offices of Kirkland & Ellis LLP. His practice focuses primarily on intellectual property litigation, including copyright, patent and trademark. His clients include both privately held and publicly traded companies from a wide range of industries, including computer software and video games, media and entertainment—such as film, music, publishing, television and theatre—personal care products, and telecommunications. Mr. Simmons is the author of several articles concerning intellectual property, and he is the vice chair of the American Bar Association's Copyright & Social Media committee. He received his B.A. from Brandeis University, and his J.D. from Columbia Law School, where he was awarded the Caroll G. Harper Prize for achievement in intellectual property and served as the Executive Editor of the *Columbia Business Law Review.*

Brittany Adkins Schaffer

Chapter 6: What May Be Protected by Copyright: Unique and Specific Applications of Copyright Law Online

Brittany Adkins Schaffer is an attorney with Loeb & Loeb, LLP, in Nashville, Tennessee, where she practices in all areas of entertainment-related intellectual property law, including corporate and licensing transactions, litigation, and counseling, primarily for clients in the music and publishing industries. Her principal clients include record labels, publishing and video production companies, management companies, recording artists, producers, songwriters, authors, and other parties in the entertainment industry. Ms. Schaffer's litigation practice focuses heavily on copyright, trademark, right of publicity, and other entertainment matters. She received her B.A., magna cum laude, from Vanderbilt University, and her J.D., magna cum laude, from Samford University, Cumberland School of Law, where she also served as Editor-In-Chief of the *Cumberland Law Review,* and published articles on copyright law and on the right of publicity. In 2012, Brittany was recognized by *Super Lawyers* as one of the "Mid-South Rising Stars" and by *Variety* magazine as one of "Hollywood's New Leaders."

Howard S. Hogan
Stephen W. Feingold

Chapters 7–8: Unique Online Trademark Issues; Domain Name Registration, Maintenance, and Protection

Howard S. Hogan is a partner in the Washington, D.C. office of Gibson, Dunn & Crutcher LLP. Mr. Hogan's practice focuses on intellectual property litigation and counseling, including trademark, copyright, patent, false advertising, right of publicity, licensing, and trade secret matters. Many of Mr. Hogan's matters have tested the application of traditional legal principles to the Internet and new media, such as issues of Internet jurisdiction, online contracting, and the application of trademark and copyright law to search engines, social media, and online sales. Mr. Hogan also regularly counsels clients in connection with the application of privacy law to online commercial activities and data breaches, and has assisted clients with several substantial trade secrets and information security matters. Mr. Hogan received his B.S.F.S., magna cum laude, in 1994 from Georgetown University School of Foreign Service where he was Phi Beta Kappa, and his J.D., cum laude, in 1999 from New York University School of Law, where he was Editor-in-Chief of *The Commentator* and Research and Writing Editor for the Moot Court Board. Mr. Hogan is also an alumnus of Lady Margaret Hall, Oxford University, where he spent the 1992–93 academic term as a visiting student. From 1999–2000, Mr. Hogan served as a Law Clerk to the Honorable Naomi Reice Buchwald, United States District Judge for the Southern District of New York. Mr. Hogan is a frequent lecturer and writer on intellectual property and technology-related issues.

Stephen W. Feingold is a partner at Kilpatrick Townsend & Stockton, LLP. His practice focuses on trademark, copyright, privacy and Internet law. Trained as a litigator, Steve is also well recognized as a leading licensing attorney and general brand consultant. During the course of his career, he has represented some of the leading consumer brands in the United States, including Pearson Education, Caesars, Schering Plough, Century 21, LukOil, Chippendales, and Merv Griffin. Recognized as a New York "Super Lawyer" for many years, Steve's contributions to the trademark bar were recognized when he was the recipient of the 2002 INTA Volunteer of the Year Award. He currently serves on the editorial boards of *The Intellectual Property Law Strategist* and *Internet Law & Strategy*. Steve is a frequent speaker and writer on Internet-related issues. He is the creator of a patent-pending Web-based application, the NAMEALIZER (TM) which helps clients identify domain name infringements that are causing true economic injury. *IP Magazine* recognized Steve's creativity and combination of legal and business acumen by naming him Runner-Up for Best Domain Name Strategy of 2010 for the NAMEALIZER(TM). He is a finalist in that same category in 2011.

Michael Ridgway Jones
Vesna N. Rafaty
Yakov Ginzburg

Chapter 9: Protection of Content in the Online Environment

Michael Ridgway Jones is an attorney with Loeb & Loeb, LLP in New York City. Mr. Jones maintains a diverse practice with a particular emphasis on representing media, telecommunications, technology, and financial services companies. He handles the negotiation of intellectual property and technology license, collaboration, joint venture, development, transition services and other agreements. He has particular experience in the areas of advanced advertising, new and emerging media (including social media), pharmaceutical licensing and collaborations, internet and mobile advertising, privacy, software and technology licensing and outsourcing. He advises clients in those areas in connection with a wide variety of legal and business issues. In addition, he assists for-profit and non-profit clients in trademark and copyright compliance, prosecution, advice and policing, as well as in advertising compliance. He supervises due diligence for patent, trademark, and copyright assets in securitizations, mergers, asset purchases and other corporate transactions in a variety of industries, including pharmaceuticals, biotechnology, information technology, financial services and video entertainment, including analysis of software development agreements and licenses. He has published and spoken on issues of copyright law and online privacy. He received a B.A. with highest honors from Emory University, a Ph.D. from Yale University, and a J.D. from Emory University, where he was an editor of the *Emory Law Journal* and a member of Order of the Coif.

Vesna N. Rafaty owns and operates an intellectual property firm based in Dallas, Texas. Clients include individuals, multimedia content producers, small businesses, artists, technology startups and device companies internationalizing into the US market. A former chemical engineer, Vesna is registered to practice before the U.S. Patent & Trademark Office and is licensed in New York and Texas. In 2010, Vesna co-founded, with the CTO of the company, a cloud computing startup that pioneered a software-as-a-service, speech-enabled, virtual contact center with a novel do-it-yourself user interface for small and medium-sized businesses.

Yakov Ginzburg is a registered patent attorney and software engineer with The Capital Group Companies, Inc., in Los Angeles, California. While in law school, Mr. Ginzburg worked full-time on design, development and support of the Web-based applications to support investment research. He has more than ten years of experience in developing large-scale custom software solutions in various industries, including Telecommunications, Entertainment, Local Government, and Financials. Before joining The Capital Group Companies, Mr. Ginzburg worked at Big 4 consulting companies Capgemini, LLC and BearingPoint, Inc. Mr. Ginzburg is also a Certified Information Systems Auditor (CISA). He graduated from Loyola Law School (JD), Los Angeles. He also holds a B.S. in Business Administration, magna cum laude, from The University of Southern California, and an M.S. in Civil Engineering from University "Lvivska Polytechnica," in Lviv, Ukraine.

David Collado
Li Dai
Stephanie Idio
Rick Sanchez

Chapter 10: Patents and the Internet

David Collado is a student at Benjamin N. Cardozo School of Law in Manhattan. He possesses undergraduate degrees in materials science and digital media, as well as an MBA. Mr. Collado's early career focused on semiconductor processing technology at Texas Instruments, which fueled his deeper passion for technological innovation. His subsequent studies in digital media, business and marketing led to careers in Web development and online marketing. This broad exposure to diverse technologies, combined with his passion for facilitating innovation, led him to law school where he plans to study the full spectrum of intellectual property law.

Li Dai is an attorney who has practiced law in both the United States and China. In the United States, she is an attorney with Ishimaru & Associates LLP in San Jose, California, a firm founded in 1997 to support the needs of clients in the electronic, semiconductor, information technology and biotechnology spaces, with a focus on patent prosecution and litigation. Before joining Ishimaru & Associates, she practiced corporate, contract and employment law in Beijing. In China, Li Dai's practice focuses on compliance, trade, investment and taxation. She received her LL.M. degree from Santa Clara University School of Law with a focus on IP law. She holds an LL.B. degree from Yanshan University in China.

Stephanie Idio is a graduate of Florida Coastal School of Law in Jacksonville, Florida, whose practice focuses on copyrights, trademarks, and technology and fashion law at The Law Office of Brittany Rawlings, P.A. Ms. Idio also works at Fashion Boss, New York, and authors her own fashion law blog at www.fashionlegallaire.blogspot.com.

Rick Sanchez has experience in the areas of patent prosecution, patent asset development & management, and patent litigation. He has a degree in electrical engineering with a minor in mathematics, coupled with several years of relevant work experience. Mr. Sanchez has served as a Cryptologic Officer in the U.S. Navy Reserve.

Richard F. O'Malley, Jr.
Griffith B. Price, Jr.
Michael C. Spillner

Chapter 11: Trade Secrets Online

Richard F. O'Malley, Jr. is a partner in Sidley Austin LLP's Chicago office. Mr. O'Malley's practice focuses on complex commercial litigation, principally in the intellectual property (patent and trade secret litigation) and class action areas. Mr. O'Malley has represented companies in a wide range of industries, including computer software, fiber optics and pharmaceutical companies. He has been successful in the state, federal district and appellate courts. He is the firm's Chicago chair of its Pro Bono and Public Interest Law Committee. He graduated summa cum laude and Phi Beta Kappa from the University of Notre Dame with a B.A. in Economics and obtained his J.D., magna cum laude, while on the Law Review at University of Illinois College of Law.

Griffith B. Price, Jr. is a member of the New York and District of Columbia Bars and is Senior Counsel with Finnegan, Henderson, Farabow, Garrett & Dunner, L.L.P., in Washington, D.C. Mr. Price has practiced in the field of intellectual property litigation for more than 35 years, focusing on trade secret, trademark and trade dress, patent infringement, false advertising, unfair competition, and related claims. He has an extensive background in damage assessment in IP litigation of all kinds, and has often written and lectured on these topics, including a series of columns on the impact of *Bilski v. Kappos* and related patentability cases, arguing for the relative advantages of trade secret protection. Mr. Price received his A.B. degree cum laude from Harvard College, and his Ll.B. degree from the New York University School of Law, where he was a Root-Tilden Scholar and Managing Editor of the *Annual Survey of American Law.* He has served on the boards of the United States Trademark Association (predecessor of the International Trademark Association) and the American Intellectual Property Law Association, on the editorial boards of *The Trademark Reporter* and the *AIPLA Quarterly Journal,* and on many committees of USTA/INTA, AIPLA, ABA IP Section, and other organizations. He is an AIPLA Fellow, and served as a member of the statutory USPTO Trademark Advisory Committee under both the Clinton and the second Bush administrations.

Michael C. Spillner is a partner in the intellectual property litigation group at Orrick, Herrington & Sutcliffe LLP, in Menlo Park, California. He has substantial experience representing both plaintiffs and defendants in trade secret disputes, including successfully defending Intel in *Silvaco Data Systems v. Intel Corp.,* 184 Cal. App. 4th 210 (2010). He was a primary drafter of the first official model jury instructions for trade secret misappropriation cases for use in California, and is an author and contributing editor of the California State Bar's treatise on trade secret misappropriation. He received his J.D. from Stanford Law School, where he served as Executive Editor of the *Stanford Law Review.* He received his undergraduate degree, summa cum laude and Phi Betta Kappa, from the University of California, Los Angeles.

Archit P. Shah
Mansi H. Shah
Andrew N. Stein

Chapter 12: Patents and the Internet

Archit P. Shah is an intellectual property litigation attorney in the Chicago office of Kirkland & Ellis LLP. He represents clients in complex

patent infringement litigation both in federal district courts and before
the U.S. International Trade Commission. He has experience in all phases of patent litigation, including portfolio analysis and pre-filing investigation; depositions of expert and fact witnesses; written discovery; claim
construction; motions practice including evidentiary and dispositive motions; preparing fact and expert witnesses for trial; assisting in direct and
cross examinations; and post-trial proceedings before the ITC and the
Federal Circuit. Mr. Shah's technical expertise includes a strong background in computer science and electrical engineering. He has advised
clients on intellectual property relating to business software, computer
graphics, virtual machines, operating systems, and Internet protocols.
Mr. Shah is also actively involved in pro bono work, focusing on representing individual clients seeking relief under Section 1983 for violations
of constitutional rights.

Mansi H. Shah is an attorney in Morgan Lewis's Litigation and Intellectual Property Practices. Ms. Shah maintains a diverse intellectual
property practice, encompassing patent and trademark litigation, client
counseling, patent and trademark prosecution, and patent-based antitrust
investigations. Ms. Shah's litigation experience spans from pre-litigation
investigation through jury and bench trials, including taking depositions; drafting early dispositive motions, discovery and pre-trial motions;
drafting claim construction, summary judgment, and post-trial motions;
managing fact and expert discovery, including working with and managing expert witnesses. Ms. Shah represents Fortune 500 companies—as
both plaintiff and defendant—in complex cases involving complex technologies. Ms. Shah maintains a client counseling and patent prosecution
practice, which includes intellectual property due diligence, and written
and oral advocacy before the U.S. Patent and Trademark Office. She has
drafted opinions of counsel related to patent infringement, validity, and
enforceability. She also has experience in patent-based antitrust investigations and cases involving design patents, trade dress, and trademarks. Ms.
Shah is the treasurer of the North American South Asian Bar Association,
the firm's associate delegate to the Coalition of Women's Initiatives in the
Law, and most served as a pupilage group co-chair for the Richard Linn
Inn of Court. Ms. Shah earned her J.D. from the George Washington University Law School in 2006, where she interned at the United States Patent
and Trade Mark Office's Board of Patent Appeals and Interferences, and
served as the Executive Notes Editor for the *American Intellectual Property
Law Association Quarterly Journal*. She earned her B.S. in computer science
from the University of California, San Diego, in 2003.

Andrew N. Stein is an attorney in the Litigation Department of Dew-
ey & LeBoeuf LLP, and is a member of its Intellectual Property Litigation
Practice. His practice focuses on intellectual property litigation in federal
district courts and on Section 337 Investigations before the U.S. International Trade Commission. Mr. Stein has represented clients in litigation
matters involving diverse technologies: computer software, automobiles,
electro-mechanical and mechanical devices, financial products and services, banking systems, cellular telephones and networks, footwear, and

LCD televisions and displays. He also served as a Special Assistant District Attorney in the Kings County (Brooklyn) District Attorney's Office through its Partners-in-Prosecution Program. During his six-month rotation with the Office, he was trial counsel for multiple jury trials and lead counsel for various pre-trial evidentiary hearings. Mr. Stein has been an active member of the AIPLA since law school, having served in many leadership roles with the organization, including an appointment to the Association's Committee on Nominations and an appointment to the Association's *Amicus* Committee. He received his J.D. from the Catholic University of America, Columbus School of Law in 2006, and his B.S. in Computer Science from the Georgia Institute of Technology in 2003.

Michael B. Smith
Sara Anne Hook
Aly Z. Dossa

Chapter 13: Intellectual Property Issues Raised by E-mail

Michael B. Smith is Senior Corporate Counsel for Latin America and Brand Protection at Sony Computer Entertainment America. He is responsible for all legal matters relating to the PlayStation® business in Latin America, including litigation, commercial transactions, business development, risk management, marketing, compliance, and intellectual property. He also is responsible protecting the PlayStation® brand throughout the Americas. Prior to joining the PlayStation® team, Mr. Smith was a commercial litigator in New York and California, with an emphasis on complex litigation involving technology, software, the Internet, and new media. Mr. Smith has represented clients in complex patent, copyright, trademark and trade secrets disputes, predominantly involving the software, semiconductor, computer, and biotechnology industries, and has significant experience litigating Section 337 investigations before the International Trade Commission. In addition, Mr. Smith has extensive experience defending companies in consumer actions arising under the CAN-SPAM Act, FTC Act and numerous state statutes concerning unsolicited, false, or deceptive marketing practices. Mr. Smith received his A.B. from Harvard College and his J.D. from Columbia University.

Sara Anne Hook is Professor of Informatics, Indiana University School of Informatics, IUPUI, where she has developed a suite of online courses in the emerging field of legal informatics. She has also served as Adjunct Professor of Law in the Indiana University School of Law–Indianapolis, where she taught courses in intellectual property law and professional responsibility. Previously, she was Associate Dean of the Faculties for IUPUI and Head Librarian at the Indiana University School of Dentistry. She holds a B.A. in History and an M.L.S. (Library Science) from the University of Michigan, an M.B.A. in Finance from the Kelley School of Business, Indiana University, and a J.D. from the Robert H. McKinney School of Law, Indiana University. Professor Hook was admitted to the Indiana bar in 1994 and to the Supreme Court of the United States in

2012. Her research interests include intellectual property law, the emerging field of legal informatics, electronic discovery, legal technology, legal research techniques, and issues related to privacy and security. She is a member of the American Intellectual Property Law Association (AIPLA), the Indiana State Bar Association, the International Legal Technology Association (ILTA), the American Association for State and Local History (AASLH) and the Rotary Club of Indianapolis.

Aly Z. Dossa is a patent attorney registered with the U.S. Patent and Trademark Office and partner with Osha Liang, L.L.P., in Houston, Texas. Mr. Dossa's practice focuses on U.S. and foreign patent prosecution, licensing, drafting and review of agreements, drafting opinions, and other intellectual property work, with an emphasis on technology areas such as business methods, computer software, and networking. He has helped clients of all sizes to establish and grow patent portfolios and formulate company-wide IP strategies. Mr. Dossa graduated from the University of Houston Law Center (J.D.) and Queen's University, Canada (B.S. Computer Science, with distinction, and B.S. Engineering Chemistry, with First Class Honors).

Dr. Michael J. Meehan

Chapter 14: The Law of Virtual Property

Michael J. Meehan, JD, PhD, is a lawyer who works at the intersection of technology, law, and business. He is a registered patent attorney and holds a JD from Stanford University, a PhD and an MS in Computer Science from the University of North Carolina, and a BSE in Computer Engineering from Purdue University. Most of this chapter was written while Dr. Meehan was a patent attorney at Knobbe Martens Olson & Bear. Dr. Meehan is currently a patent lawyer in Mountain View, California and serves on the Advisory Boards of InnerOptic Technology, Inc and Dorsata, Inc. Before entering the legal profession, Dr. Meehan was a researcher at Stanford University, working in the field of virtual and computer-assisted surgery, and helped lead computer science start-ups. Dr. Meehan served as a clerk to the Honorable William C. Bryson on the U.S. Court of Appeals for the Federal Circuit.

Summary Table of Contents

Part III
Protecting the Key Elements of a Web Site

Part IV
Issues Arising From Conducting Business Online

Detailed Table of Contents

PART I
INTELLECTUAL PROPERTY IMPLICATIONS OF
USING ONLINE NAVIGATING TOOLS

PART III
PROTECTING THE KEY ELEMENTS OF A WEB SITE

Part I

Intellectual Property Implications of Using Online Navigating Tools

1

Search Engines

G. Peter Albert
AlbertDhand, LLP
San Diego, California

Rita Abbati
Director and Counsel
ConnectMed International
San Diego, California

II. Implications of Using Another's Mark as a Metatag or Keyword

B. Can Metatags and Keywords Create Consumer Confusion?

3. *A Circuit-by-Circuit Perspective*

a. *Ninth Circuit*

[Add the following text following the first paragraph on page 26.]

One Ninth Circuit decision involving the sale of a trademark by search engines (most prominently via Google's AdWords and through Microsoft's Bing) to trigger links sponsored by a competitor distinctly rejected the application of the "Internet trinity" or "troika" espoused by earlier cases as the test for trademark infringement. In *Network Automation, Inc. v. Advanced Systems Concepts, Inc.,*[1] the court recognized that the

---

[1]638 F.3d 1137, 97 USPQ2d 2036 (9th Cir. 2011) (vacating an injunction that prohibited defendant Network Automation from advertising its product by purchasing certain keywords matching plaintiff's trademarks which would produce a search results page showing www.NetworkAutomation.com as a sponsored link).

"troika" factors first appeared in the *Brookfield* case to analyze the risk of source confusion generated by similar domain names, and that the Ninth Circuit has subsequently found the "troika" helpful to resolve disputes involving Web sites with similar names or appearances.[2] However, given the "multifaceted nature of the Internet and the ever-expanding ways in which we all use the technology … it makes no sense to prioritize the same three factors for every type of potential online commercial activity. The 'troika' is a particularly poor fit for the question presented here."[3]

This court also specified that in "examin[ing] initial interest confusion, the owner of the mark must demonstrate likely confusion, not mere diversion."[4]

[Add the following new section.]

4.   *Revisiting Likelihood of Confusion for Trademark Uses as Keywords [New Topic]*

In *Rosetta Stone Ltd. v. Google, Inc.*,[5] a Fourth Circuit court recently revisited the question of whether using trademarks to trigger sponsored links can cause *actual* confusion.

Rosetta Stone is a leading language-learning software manufacturer. In 2009, Rosetta Stone sued Google for sale of the Rosetta Stone trademarks as part of its AdWords program which generates sponsored links to the Web sites of paying advertisers. The district court entered summary judgment against Rosetta Stone's claims for direct, contributory, and vicarious trademark infringement and against its dilution claims. The Fourth Circuit reversed the summary judgment rulings in Google's favor on the direct infringement, contributory infringement, and dilution claims.

The court's analysis of the direct infringement claim is of particular interest because of the way in which it evaluated the evidence of actual confusion and intent. While the evidence may not have presented actual *source* confusion, it did present actionable confusion as to *affiliation, connection or sponsorship*.[6] The district court had dismissed the testimony of five

_____

[2] *Id.* at 1148, 97 USPQ2d at 2043. For a discussion of cases, see text at notes 116–128 in the main volume. *See also* Internet Specialties West, Inc. v. Milon-DiGiorgio Enters., Inc., 559 F.3d 985, 989, 90 USPQ2d 1151, 1153 (9th Cir. 2009); Perfumebay.com, Inc. v. eBay, Inc., 506 F.3d 1165, 1169, 1173, 84 USPQ2d 1865, 1868, 1871 (9th Cir. 2007); Interstellar Starship Servs., Ltd. v. Epix, Inc., 304 F.3d 936, 942, 64 USPQ2d 1514, 1518 (9th Cir. 2002); GoTo. com, Inc. v. Walt Disney Co., 202 F.3d 1199, 1205, 53 USPQ2d 1652, 1656 (9th Cir. 2000).

[3] *Network Automation*, 638 F.3d at 1148–49, 97 USPQ2d at 2043. The court cited Jonathan Moskin, *Virtual Trademark Use—The Parallel World of Keyword Ads*, 98 TRADEMARK REP. 873, 892–93 (2008), which argued that "the 'troika' is inadequate for analyzing trademark infringement claims based on search engine keyword advertising because it omits important factors." *Network Automation*, 638 F.3d at 1149, 97 USPQ2d at 2043.

[4] *Id.*, 97 USPQ2d at 2043.

[5] 730 F. Supp. 2d 531, 97 USPQ2d 1855 (E.D. Va. 2010), *aff'd in part, vacated in part, and remanded*, 676 F.3d 144, 102 USPQ2d 1473 (4th Cir. 2012).

[6] *Id.*, 676 F.3d at 157, 102 USPQ2d at 1482.

consumers who had used sponsored links on the Google search page to purchase counterfeit Rosetta Stone software,[7] as well as an expert report that showed significant consumer confusion about whether sponsored links were authorized or approved by Rosetta Stone.[8] In contrast, the appellate court found these pieces of evidence to be probative of confusion as to affiliation, connection or sponsorship—even though the purchasers knew they were not purchasing directly from Rosetta Stone's Web site.[9] In addition, there appeared to be some evidence of actual *source* confusion as well which the district court had dismissed. Rosetta Stone had received more than 250 complaints from consumers who were allegedly misled into buying counterfeit software over the course of eleven months.[10] In addition, Google's in-house attorneys themselves were not able to identify whether a sponsored link was by an authorized reseller or an unauthorized advertiser/competitor.[11] The court observed that such "'uncertain[ty about] the origin' of a product ... is quintessential actual confusion evidence."[12]

Regarding evidence of intent, the Fourth Circuit found incriminating Google's about-face regarding its policy on allowing advertisers to use others' trademarks not only as keywords but in the text of the sponsored links. Prior to 2004, Google did not allow the use of trademarks as keyword search triggers at all. In 2004, Google loosened its restrictions on the use of trademarks as keywords to "[p]rovide users with more choice and greater access to relevant information."[13] At that time, however, Google "continue[d] to prevent advertisers from using ... trademarks in their *ad text* or *ad titles* unless the advertiser is authorized to do so by the trademark owner"—likely because internal studies performed by Google at the time "suggested that there was significant source confusion among Internet searchers when trademarks were included in the title or body of the advertisements."[14] Nonetheless, Google shifted its policy in 2009, allowing some use of trademarks in the text or title of the sponsored link even without ownership or approval.[15] With this change in policy, Google expected both "a substantial boost in revenue from ... as well as an uptick in litigation from trademark owners."[16] Because Google did not conduct any further studies to contradict its earlier position that confusion was

---

[7] *Id.* at 156–57, 102 USPQ2d at 1481–82.

[8] *Id.* at 159, 102 USPQ2d at 1484.

[9] *Id.* at 157, 102 USPQ2d at 1482.

[10] *Id.* at 157–58, 102 USPQ2d at 1483.

[11] *Id.* at 158–59, 102 USPQ2d at 1483–84.

[12] *Id.*, 102 USPQ2d at 1483 (citing Sara Lee Corp. v. Kayser-Roth Corp., 81 F.3d 455, 466, 38 USPQ2d 1449, 1457 (4th Cir. 1996)).

[13] *Id.* at 155, 102 USPQ2d at 1481.

[14] *Id.* at 156, 102 USPQ2d at 1481 (emphasis added).

[15] Google informed customers and potential customers that it was "adjusting [its] trademark policy ... to allow some ads to use trademarks in the ad text. Under certain criteria, you can use trademark terms in your ad text ... even if you don't own that trademark or have explicit approval from the trademark owner to use it." *Id.*, 102 USPQ2d at 1481.

[16] *Id.*, 102 USPQ2d at 1481.

very likely to result from its use of the marks, the court held that "a reasonable trier of fact could find that Google intended to cause confusion in that it acted with the knowledge that confusion was very likely to result from its use of the marks."[17]

The summary judgment ruling on the dilution claims in Google's favor was also reversed as to (1) the district court's conclusion that Rosetta Stone "was required but failed to present evidence that Google was 'us[ing] the Rosetta Stone Marks to identify its *own* goods and services,'"[18] and (2) the district court's conclusion that Rosetta Stone failed to show that "Google's use of the mark was likely to impair the distinctiveness of or harm the reputation of the ROSETTA STONE marks."[19]

As to the district court's first finding, the appellate court held that the lower court erred by placing the burden on Rosetta Stone to demonstrate that Google was using the Rosetta Stone marks as a source identifier for Google's own products. Instead,

> once the owner of a famous mark establishes a prima facie case of dilution by blurring or tarnishment, it falls to the defendant to demonstrate that its use constituted a "fair use ... other than as a designation of source for the [defendant's] own goods or services," 15 U.S.C. §1125(c)(3)(A). Whether Google used the mark other than as a source identifier and in good faith is an issue that Google, not Rosetta Stone, is obligated to establish.[20]

Moreover, the district court erred when it ruled that Google was not liable for dilution simply because there was no evidence that Google used the Rosetta Stone marks to identify Google's own goods and services. "In essence, the district court made nontrademark use coextensive with the 'fair use' defense under the [Federal Trademark Dilution Act] FTDA. The statute, however, requires more than showing that defendant's use was 'other than as a designation of source'—the defendant's use must also qualify as a 'fair use.' 15 U.S.C. §1125(c)(3)(A)."[21] The summary judgment conclusion omitted the traditional "fair use" analysis established by previous cases, "impermissibly omitting the question of good faith and collapsing the fair-use defense into one question—whether or not Google uses the ROSETTA STONE mark as a source identifier for its own products."[22]

The appellate court next considered the district court's second finding that Google's use was not likely to impair or harm the Rosetta Stone marks where there was "'no evidence of dilution by blurring when Rosetta Stone's brand awareness has only increased since Google revised its trademark policy in 2004'" and where "'Rosetta Stone's brand awareness equity also increased from 19% in 2005 to 95% in 2009.'"[23] The district

---

[17] *Id.*, 102 USPQ2d at 1481.

[18] *Id.* at 168, 102 USPQ2d at 1491 (quoting 730 F. Supp. 2d at 551, 97 USPQ2d at 1869) (emphasis in original).

[19] *Id.*, 102 USPQ2d at 1491.

[20] *Id.* at 168–69, 102 USPQ2d at 1491.

[21] *Id.* at 169, 102 USPQ2d at 1491.

[22] *Id.* at 170–71, 102 USPQ2d at 1492.

[23] *Id.* at 168, 102 USPQ2d at 1491 (quoting 730 F. Supp. 2d at 551, 97 USPQ2d at 1870).

court had relied heavily on a holding from a factually different case that "'no claim for dilution by blurring exists where a defendants' [*sic*] product only increases public identification of the plaintiffs' marks.'"[24] There are several likelihood-of-dilution factors enumerated under the FTDA, and the district court improperly focused only on the inquiry as to whether Rosetta Stone had suffered actual injury to its brand.[25]

The issue of dilution in this case will rest on the question on remand: whether Rosetta Stone's marks became famous *after* Google's sale of the marks as keyword began creating a likelihood of confusion.[26] Rosetta Stone's claim would fail under the record before the district court, which established that Rosetta Stone's marks had become famous in 2009, *after* Google's sale of trademarks began in 2004.

However, this case may only establish that the Fourth Circuit is a more favorable forum for plaintiffs involving keywords and sponsored links. Related cases from the Ninth Circuit have held that using trademarks as keywords do not cause consumer confusion:

> [I]n the age of FIOS, cable modems, DSL and T1 lines, reasonable, prudent and experienced internet consumers are accustomed to such exploration by trial and error. They skip from site to site, ready to hit the back button whenever they're not satisfied with a site's contents. They fully expect to find some sites that aren't what they imagine based on a glance at the domain name or search engine summary. Outside the special case of ... domains that actively claim affiliation with the trademark holder, consumers don't form any firm expectations about the sponsorship of a website until they've seen the landing page—if then.[27]

---

[24] *Id.* at 168, 170, 102 USPQ2d at 1491, 1493 (quoting 730 F. Supp. 2d at 551, 97 USPQ2d at 1870 (citing Louis Vuitton Malletier S.A. v. Haute Diggity Dog, LLC, 507 F.3d 252, 264, 84 USPQ2d 1969, 1978 (4th Cir. 2007))).

[25] *Id.* at 170, 102 USPQ2d at 1492–93.

[26] *Id.* at 172–73, 102 USPQ2d at 1494.

[27] Toyota Motor Sales, U.S.A. v. Tabari, 610 F.3d 1171, 1179, 95 USPQ2d 1702, 1708 (9th Cir. 2010) (vacating an injunction that prohibited a pair of automobile brokers from using Toyota's "Lexus" mark in their domain names.); Network Automation, Inc. v. Advanced Sys. Concepts, Inc., 638 F.3d 1137, 1153, 97 USPQ2d 2036, 2046 (9th Cir. 2011) (vacating an injunction that prohibited defendant Network Automation from advertising its product by purchasing certain keywords matching plaintiff's trademarks which would produce a search results page showing www.NetworkAutomation.com as a sponsored link) (discussed in Section II.B.3.a, *supra*, this supplement).

2

Links and Frames

G. Peter Albert, Jr.
AlbertDhand, LLP
San Diego, California

Rita Abbati
Director and Counsel
ConnectMed International
San Diego, California

III. Copyright Implications of Linking and Framing

B. Indirect Copyright Liability for In-line Linking

[Add the following text at the end of the first full paragraph on page 95.]

In contrast, the court in *Flava Works, Inc. v. Gunter*[1] made it clear that the *Perfect 10 v. Google* decision was highly fact-specific and therefore inapplicable to that case. Plaintiff Flava Works produced and distributed adult entertainment videos. Defendant myVidster.com's users copied and/or posted copyrighted works belonging to Flava Works without authorization. Most of the users did not back up the copyrighted videos on the site, but directed myVidster.com to "embed" video clips on the site through the posting/bookmarking process, which the defendants likened to in-line linking. The defendants asserted that *Perfect 10* stands for the proposition that anyone who links to a third-party site cannot be liable for direct copyright infringement.[2]

The defendants argued that the videos posted to myVidster were hosted on third-party servers, as were the full-size images in *Perfect 10,* and "the way the videos are linked and displayed is the same as in *Perfect 10*"[3] because they were shown to the viewer as if they were part of the myVidster site, even though the videos were hosted by (stored on) a third-party server. The court did not agree that both cases use "essentially the same technology."[4]

> Both cases may involve inline linking, but the processes are quite different. The relevant comparison is between the conduct of Google and the conduct of myVidster's users, not between Google and myVidster. In response to a search query, Google's image search engine uses an automated process to display search results through inline linking. In contrast, myVidster's users do not employ any sort of automation to determine which videos they bookmark; rather, they personally select and submit videos for inline linking/embedding on myVidster. (And many of those hand-picked videos are infringing.)[5]

Moreover, the fact that the majority of the videos displayed on myVidster resided on a third-party server was not dispositive. MyVidster users caused a "display" to be made by bookmarking those videos, which display could simply be initiated by going to a myVidster URL and clicking "play."[6] Unlike the full-size images in *Perfect 10 v. Google,* the user could navigate to a collection of myVidster videos and did not have to go to each separate source site to completely view them.[7]

---

[1] No. 10 C 6517, 2011 WL 3876910, 2011 U.S. Dist. LEXIS 98451 (N.D. Ill. Sept. 1, 2011).

[2] *Id.* at *1, 2011 U.S. Dist. LEXIS 98451, at *4.

[3] *Id.* at *2, 2011 U.S. Dist. LEXIS 98451, at *9.

[4] *Id.*, 2011 U.S. Dist. LEXIS 98451, at *10.

[5] *Id.* at *4, 2011 U.S. Dist. LEXIS 98451, at *10 (footnote omitted) (emphasis in original).

[6] *Id.* at *4, 2011 U.S. Dist. LEXIS 98451, at *11.

[7] *Id.*, 2011 U.S. Dist. LEXIS 98451, at *11.

3

Web Crawlers

Stephen Weed*
RatnerPrestia
Valley Forge, Pennsylvania

II. TRESPASS TO CHATTELS CLAIMS

A. Applying the Trespass Tort in the Electronic World

[Add the following text at the beginning of the section.]

Whether the common law tort of trespass to chattels can be applied to the electronic world at all is an initial question. After all, "chattel," by definition, refers to physical, not intangible, property.[1] The vocabulary of the World Wide Web has, ab initio, been rooted in the physical, real, off-line world: a "home" page is part of a Web "site" that one can "visit." But

---

*Wendy Leibowitz of Bloomberg BNA drafted the trespass to chattels section.

[1] "Chattel: an item of *tangible* movable or immovable property, except real estate and things (as buildings) connected with real property." Merriam-Webster.com (*available at* http://www.merriam-webster.com/dictionary/chattel) (Aug. 31, 2012) (emphasis added).

merely because these analogies to real property and physical trespass "*can* be made does not suggest, however, that they *should* be made."[2]

In his article discussing what he calls "the ancient doctrine" of trespass to chattels as applied to Web sites, Professor I. Trotter Hardy analyzes four branches of legal property theory and applies them, successfully, to Web sites. First, under the natural property rights of John Locke's philosophy, Web site owners derive their rights from the labor they invested in creating and maintaining their property.[3] Second, Jeremy Bentham utilitarian rights theory would support the notion that it is useful for states to construct and grant artificial property rights that allow owners to restrict access to their properties through locks, fences, and guns: control can enhance the pleasure of ownership.[4] Third, Garrett Hardin's "tragedy of the commons" acknowledges that many individuals can use a site at one time, akin to a public gathering place, but a Web site, which depends on communicating over networks, can become overloaded, impeding access to present and future users, and so access to those who abuse the commons can be barred.[5]

Finally, under Professor Margaret Jane Radin's "property as personhood" theory,[6] in which an owner values a piece of property, such as a wedding ring, a house, or a photograph, over another, more fungible, commodity, a Web site expresses the individual personality of an owner, including a corporate owner, and thus could be considered property worthy of protection under the legal rule against trespasses. Thus, Professor Hardy states, these "[f]our strands of property theory ... turn out to yield strong justifications for treating Web sites as property and hence for the application to them of the common law of trespass."[7]

Indeed, early claims of trespass to chattels met with success in court, particularly as Internet service providers sought to combat spam, the unsolicited commercial e-mail that harmed their networks.[8] Such claims

---

[2] I. Trotter Hardy, *The Ancient Doctrine of Trespass to Web Sites*, 1996 J. ONLINE LAW, art. 7, ¶1 (hereinafter Hardy) (*available at* http://scholarship.law.wm.edu/facpubs/1198) (emphasis in original). Professor Hardy notes that physical trespass claims appear incongruous in cyberspace, since technical means can frequently be used to bar or limit unwanted visitors. *Id.* at ¶4.

[3] *Id.* at ¶¶24–29 (citing JOHN LOCKE, SECOND TREATISE OF GOVERNMENT, *reprinted in* C.B. MACPHERSON, EDITOR, PROPERTY: MAINSTREAM AND CRITICAL POSITIONS (1978)).

[4] *Id.* at ¶¶30–37 (citing JEREMY BENTHAM, THE THEORY OF LEGISLATION (Oceana Pubs. 1975)).

[5] *Id.* at ¶¶38–48.

[6] *Id.* at ¶¶49–52 (citing MARGARET JANE RADIN, REINTERPRETING PROPERTY (1993)).

[7] *Id.* at ¶1. For a contrary perspective, see Dan L. Burk, *The Trouble With Trespass*, 4 J. SMALL & EMERGING BUS. L. 27 (2000). Burk argues that in *Thrifty-Tel, Inc. v. Bezenek* (see Section II of the main volume), CompuServe, Inc. v. Cyber Promotions, Inc., 962 F. Supp. 1015 (S.D. Ohio 1997), and Intel Corp. v. Hamidi, No. 98 AS05067, 1999 WL 450944 (Cal. App. Dep't Super. Ct. Apr. 28, 1999), courts misapplied the law of trespass, and asserts that the law of nuisance is more appropriate to these kinds of electronic offenses.

[8] *See, e.g.,* CompuServe, Inc. v. Cyber Promotions, Inc., 962 F. Supp. 1015 (S.D. Ohio 1997) (granting preliminary injunction because unsolicited email constituted a trespass to chattels); America On-Line, Inc. v. IMS, 24 F. Supp. 2d 548 (E.D. Va. 1998) (following *CompuServ*, granting summary judgment on trespass to chattels grounds); America On-

are sometimes now routinely considered trespass to chattels claims, even when originally asserted under different causes of action. For example, in *Davidoff v. Davidoff*,[9] a New York court reclassified claims of destruction of personal property, computer trespass, and computer tampering as claims for trespass to chattels.

But with the advent of anti-spam laws, the use of trespass to chattels claims has been called into question. In *Jaynes v. Commonwealth of Virginia*,[10] the Supreme Court of Virginia found the lower court had erred in construing Virginia's anti-spam law as a trespass statute to which the First Amendment would not apply. The state's statute prohibited only the intentional use of false routing information to send unsolicited commercial messages through privately owned servers in Virginia. The sender in this case was not unauthorized; the claims were not asserted against private individuals, but concerned government actors, and Virginia's anti-spam law was found to be overbroad, violating the sender's right to anonymous free speech.

Still, the trespass to chattels claim was successfully asserted against someone who shared a user name and password with a third party, even though the Web site performance was not impaired in any way. In *State Analysis, Inc. v. American Financial Services Association*,[11] the plaintiff owned a subscription-based Web site, and one of its subscribers allegedly shared a user name and password. The federal district court in Virginia found that this action alone, which allowed unauthorized access to the Web site, could support a trespass to chattels claim.

Usually, however, some damage to the service or site is required to support a trespass to chattels claim. In *School of Visual Arts v. Kuprewicz*,[12] the plaintiffs alleged that the defendant caused "large volumes" of unsolicited job applications and pornographic e-mails to be sent to the plaintiffs by way of the plaintiffs' computer system, without their consent. These e-mails depleted hard disk space, drained processing power, and adversely affected other system resources on the plaintiffs' computer system. This tortious conduct—the sending of unsolicited content, and causing a depletion or deletion of information, thereby adversely affecting the effectiveness of his Web site—constituted a claim for trespass of chattel.

Line, Inc. v. LCGM, Inc., 46 F. Supp. 2d 444 (E.D. Va. 1998) (same); America Online, Inc. v. Prime Data Sys., Inc., No. 97-1652-A, 1998 U.S. Dist. LEXIS 20226 (E.D. Va. Nov. 20, 1998) (entering default judgment on trespass to chattels grounds).

[9] 12 Misc. 3d 1162A, 819 N.Y.S.2d 209 (2006) (dismissing the case on jurisdictional grounds, since the act of damaging a Web site occurred in Florida, where defendants were located when they typed on their computer and accessed the Web site's host in Florida).

[10] 276 Va. 443, 666 S.E. 2d 303 (2008).

[11] 621 F. Supp. 2d 309 (E.D. Va. 2009).

[12] 3 Misc. 3d 278, 771 N.Y.S.2d 804 (2003). *Accord* Najieb v. William Chrysler-Plymouth, No. 01 C 8295, 2002 WL 31906466, at *10–11, 2002 U.S. Dist. LEXIS 24927, at *39 (N.D. Ill. Dec. 31, 2002) (damages are a required element of trespass to chattels claim); DirectTV, Inc. v. Jae Sun Chin, No. SA-03-CA-0660, 2003 WL 22102144, at *2, 2003 U.S. Dist. LEXIS 15815, at *7 (W.D. Tex. Aug. 26, 2003) (trespass to chattels claim dismissed because, even though time and resources were spent to delete pop-up advertisements, no facts supported damage).

III. TERMS OF USE

A.   Web Crawlers and "Browse Wrap" Agreements

[Add the following text after the first text paragraph ending in footnote 125 on page 120.]

Subsequently, in a 2012 decision,[13] the court found that Power did in fact circumvent technical barriers and, thus, its access of the Facebook Web site was "without permission." Evidence introduced in the case indicated that Power knew that Facebook would try to add technical barriers blocking their access, but that its Web crawler was designed to circumvent blocks that Facebook might impose.[14] Power argued that its access was not without permission because when Facebook did insert a technical block, "Power did not undertake any effort to circumvent that block, and did not provide users with any tools designed to circumvent it."[15] Ruling that Power's access was "without permission," the court found "no reason to distinguish between methods of circumvention built into a software system to render barriers ineffective and those which respond to barriers after they have been imposed."[16]

[Add the following text at the end of the section.]

Applying *Cvent*, the Central Division of the Utah District Court, in *Koch Industries, Inc. v. John Does, 1-25*,[17] stated that for "a plausible claim under [the CFAA], one must be guilty of gaining 'unauthorized access' or 'exceeding authorized access' to a protected computer system."[18]

In *Koch*, the defendants created a hoax Web site using information obtained from public information on Koch's Web site.[19] Koch asserted that in creating the fake Web site, the defendants acted without authorization and inconsistent with the company's grant of access found in their Web site's Terms of Use.[20] Koch argued that even if the defendants had some limited authorization to access their Web site, they acted beyond the authorization granted by breaching the Web site's Terms of Use.[21]

Comparing Koch's Web site to the Web site in *Cvent*, the court noted that like Cvent's Web site, Koch's Web site was not password protected, nor were users of the Web site required to manifest assent to the Terms of Use, such as by clicking 'I agree' before gaining access to the database;

---

[13]Facebook, Inc. v. Power Ventures, Inc., 844 F. Supp. 2d 1025 (N.D. Cal. 2012).
[14]*Id.* at 1038.
[15]*Id.*
[16]*Id.*
[17]No. 2:10CV1275DAK, 2011 U.S. Dist. LEXIS 49529 (C.D. Utah May 9, 2011).
[18]*Id.* at *20.
[19]*Id.*
[20]*Id.*
[21]*Id.*

anyone could access and search the information at will; and the Terms of Use did not appear in the body of the first page of Web site.[22] Based on these factors, the court concluded the Web site was not protected in any meaningful sense by its Terms of Use or otherwise.[23]

Ruling for the defendants, the court reasoned that because the defendants created a mock-up of Koch's Web site using information that Koch made publicly available on the Internet, without requiring any log-in, password, or other individualized grant of access, by definition, the defendants could not have exceeded their authority to access that data.[24]

Addressing policy considerations, the court stated "[i]f Koch's legal theory is correct, then any violation of its Terms of Use—that is, any use of its website's content of which Koch does not approve—could expose a political critic to criminal prosecution" and that "[s]uch a result is clearly beyond Congress' intent in passing the CFAA."[25] Recharacterizing Koch's complaint, the court stated "Koch's complaint is not that Defendants obtained the information without authorization, but rather that they ultimately used the information in an unwanted manner."[26] The court additionally stated that the "CFAA addresses only the act of trespassing or breaking into a protected computer system; it does not purport to regulate the various uses to which information may be put."[27]

---

[22] *Id.* at *21.
[23] *Id.* at *22.
[24] *Id.*
[25] *Id.* at *23–24.
[26] *Id.* at *22.
[27] *Id.*

PART II

POSTING AND USING MATERIALS ONLINE

4

Using and Protecting Copyrighted Works on the Internet

Scott Pink
DLA Piper US, LLP
Sacramento, California

I. The "Virtual" Copyright

B. Statutory Requirements for Copyright Protection

4. *What Is NOT Protectable as a Copyright*

c. *The Case of Computer Programs*

[Add the following text at the end of the section.]

A more recent application of the idea/expression dichotomy is the decision of the United States District Court for the Northern District of California in *Oracle America v. Google*.[1] In that case, the court considered the copyrightability of an application programming interface (API). An API allows programs to interact with each other. An example of an API is one written by Google for its Google Maps site that allows other programs to send requests to generate interactive maps with store locations flagged.

Oracle America v. Google involved the Android operating system for mobile devices that Google had created using Java, an open-source programming language created by Sun [later acquired by Oracle]. The Java API included 166 packages, containing hundreds of programs which accomplished thousands of tasks. Google selected 37 packages to use in its Android operating system and replicated the exact names and exact functions of virtually all of these 37 packages, but took care to use different code to implement the six thousand-plus tasks and programs. It did so to promote interoperability with previous programs written for Java.

Oracle claimed that by copying the Java API in this manner, Google had infringed its copyright in its API. The case required the district court to consider as a threshold matter whether the replicated elements were copyrightable. The district court's decision contains an excellent review of the case law involving the copyrightability of computer programs. The court initially noted that Oracle was not entitled to copyright protection in the methods or functions that were carried out by the Java API since

---

[1]No. 10-03561, 2012 WL 1964523, 2012 U.S. Dist. LEXIS 75896, 103 USPQ2d 1023 (N.D. Cal. May 31, 2012).

such methods and functions are not protectable under Section 102(b) of the Copyright Act. The court further noted that the "method specification as set forth in the declaration"—essentially the words or syntax used to call a particular function—was not copyrightable because using the words or syntax was the only way to call the function using the Java API. As the court stated:

> Significantly, when there is only one way to write something, the merger doctrine bars anyone from claiming exclusive copyright ownership of that expression. Therefore, there can be no copyright violation in using the identical declarations. Nor can there be any copyright violation due to the *name* given to the method (or to the arguments), for under the law, names and short phrases cannot be copyrighted.[2]

This left the court to consider the remaining argument—i.e., that Java's overall system of organized names—covering 37 packages, with over six hundred classes, with over six thousand names—was a "taxonomy" and therefore copyrightable under the ruling *American Dental Association v. Delta Dental Plans Association*.[3] In *American Dental*, the Seventh Circuit held that the American Dental Association's ("ADA") codes for dental procedures, could be copyrighted as a taxonomy because there was creativity and originality in how the taxonomy selected, organized, and arranged the underlying data (dental procedures). This meant that others could not slavishly copy and distribute ADA's taxonomy as a whole. However, because the underlying facts (dental procedures) represented by the taxonomy were not protected by copyright law, the ADA could not block others from using their codes to submit claims because that constituted a functional use of the taxonomy.

The court in the *Google* case distinguished the Java API from the taxonomy in *American Dental Association* because they operated a system of commands to carry out specified computer functions. Since the use of the taxonomy of the Java API was necessary to invoke the underlying functions, the court also likened them to "interface procedures for compatibility," which had been held by prior Ninth Circuit decisions to be functional aspects of software programs and not copyrightable.[4] The court thus concluded that the Java API at issue here were a method of operation and not copyrightable under Section 102(b) of the Copyright Act.

It was also significant here that Google had not simply copied the entire Java taxonomy. It only used a relatively small of the subset of the API and wrote its own code to implement each of the API functions at issue. This led the court to conclude that no infringement had occurred.[5]

---

[2] 2012 U.S. Dist. LEXIS 75896, at *73–74, 103 USPQ2d at 1042 (emphasis in original).

[3] 126 F.3d 977, 44 USPQ2d 1296 (7th Cir. 1997).

[4] *See, e.g.,* Sega Enters. Ltd. v. Accolade, Inc., 977 F.2d 1510, 24 USPQ2d 1561 (9th Cir. 1992); *see also* Sony Computer Entm't, Inc. v. Connectix Corp., 203 F.3d 596, 53 USPQ2d 1705 (9th Cir. 2000) (following *Sega Enters.*).

[5] *Oracle Am., Inc.,* 2012 WL 1964523, 2012 U.S. Dist. LEXIS 75896, at *74.

C. The Extent and Limitations of Copyright Holders' Exclusive Rights

4. Limitation: The First Sale Doctrine and Constraints on Right to Reproduce

[Add the following text after the second sentence of the first paragraph of the section on page 147.]

An unresolved question is whether the first sale doctrine applies to foreign-made copyrighted works. The issue arises when a company attempts to import foreign-made goods into the United States without permission of the copyright holder. Copyright holders are often concerned by importation of such "grey market" goods because they are often purchased at a lower price than the goods imported by licensed importers and perhaps may have different qualities and characteristics due to the markets in which they were initially sold.

Section 602(a)(1) of the Copyright Act[6] prohibits the importation into the United States of copies (or phonorecords) of copyrighted works acquired abroad without the authorization of the copyright holder. However, the question is whether the Section 602(a)(1) prohibition applies if the importer lawfully acquired a copy of the copyrighted work abroad. The argument that an importer would make is that under the first sale doctrine, the purchase of the copy extinguishes the copyright holder's right to control further disposition of that work, including exportation to the United States.

The Supreme Court had previously considered the application of Section 109(a)[7] and Section 602(a)(1) in the case of *Quality King Distributors, Inc. v. L'Anza Research International, Inc.*[8] *Quality King* involved a round trip importation: a product was manufactured in the United States, sold to an authorized foreign distributor, sold to unidentified third parties overseas, and then imported back into the United States (to sell at discounted prices) without the copyright owner's permission. The Court held that the first sale doctrine could provide a defense to an action in this context because the goods were manufactured in the United States and therefore there was no issue of the extraterritorial application of U.S. copyright law.[9] The Court expressly stated that it was not resolving a case in which the allegedly infringing imports were manufactured abroad, but indicated in dicta that copyrighted material manufactured abroad cannot be subject to the first sale doctrine.[10]

---

[6] 17 U.S.C. §602(a)(1).

[7] *Id.* §109(a) ("… the owner of a particular copy or phonorecord lawfully made under this title, or any person authorized by such owner, is entitled, without the authority of the copyright owner, to sell or otherwise dispose of the possession of that copy or phonorecord….").

[8] 523 U.S. 135, 45 USPQ2d 1961 (1998).

[9] *Id.* at 145 n.14, 45 USPQ2d at 1965 n.14.

[10] *Id.* at 148, 45 USPQ2d 1967.

The application of the first sale doctrine to foreign produced goods was first considered by the Ninth Circuit in *Omega S.A. v. Costco Wholesale Corp.*[11] Omega manufactured its watches outside the United States and sold them overseas to authorized distributors. Costco had entered into agreements with Latin American distributors to purchase Omega watches and import them into the United States for sale at their warehouse stores. Omega sued Costco to stop this practice, claiming the importation of its watches infringed its copyright in the watch design because it had not authorized such importation. Costco claimed that it was not liable for infringement because it was permitted to import the watches under the first sale doctrine.[12]

The Ninth Circuit rejected this defense finding that the doctrine applied only to goods "lawfully made under this title," meaning goods that were manufactured in the United States. Since the watches were not made under the laws of the United States, the first sale doctrine could not apply, unless those copies had already been sold in the United States with the permission of the copyright holder.[13] The decision was appealed to the Supreme Court, which affirmed in a 4-4 decision by an equally divided Court which did not resolve the issue.[14]

In a subsequent decision, the Second Circuit in *John Wiley & Sons v. Kirtsaeng,*[15] held similarly that the first sale doctrine did not apply to goods manufactured abroad by the patent holder's subsidiary if they were imported without the U.S. manufacturer's consent. The defendant, Mr. Kirtsaeng, was a college student from Thailand attending school in the United States. He had his friends and family purchase popular textbooks in Thailand for him to resell via eBay and other such sites in the United States. Each book was manufactured overseas under an agreement with the U.S. publisher and contained a printed page indicating they were for sale outside the United States only.[16] The publisher of the books, John Wiley & Sons, argued that Mr. Kirtsaeng's importation of the books violated Section 602(a)(1) of the Copyright Act. The Second Circuit held that the first sale doctrine in Section 109(a) only applies to domestically manufactured works and does not apply in any circumstances to foreign made works. It disagreed with the Ninth Circuit's holding in *Omega* that it could apply to foreign manufactured works, even if they were sold in the United States.[17]

This split in the decisions of the circuit courts apparently prompted the Supreme Court to grant certiorari to review the *Kirtsaeng* decision. It is hoped that the Supreme Court's decision will definitely resolve the application of the first sale doctrine to foreign made goods.

---

[11]541 F.3d 982, 88 USPQ2d 1102 (9th Cir. 2008).

[12]*Id.* at 984, 88 USPQ2d at 1104.

[13]*Id.* at 985–86, 88 USPQ2d at 1105–06.

[14]Costco Wholesale Corp. v. Omega, S.A., 131 S. Ct. 565, 178 L. Ed. 2d 470, 96 USPQ2d 2025 (2010).

[15]654 F.3d 210, 99 USPQ2d 1641 (2d Cir. 2011), *cert. granted,* 132 S. Ct. 1905, 182 L. Ed. 2d 770 (2012).

[16]*Id.* at 213, 99 USPQ2d at 1642.

[17]*Id.* at 221, 99 USPQ2d at 1648.

II. COPYRIGHT INFRINGEMENT: HOW ARE COPYRIGHTS ENFORCED ONLINE?

A. Meaning of Online Copyright Infringement

2. *Ownership*

[Add the following text after the penultimate sentence of the section on page 150.]

While copyright registration is generally considered a prerequisite to filing a copyright infringement claim, the Supreme Court in *Reed Elsevier, Inc. v. Muchnick*[18] considered whether a class action settlement involving both registered and unregistered copyrights could be challenged for lack of registration. The Supreme Court held that the lower courts had jurisdiction to enter the settlement because Section 411(a) is not a grant of jurisdiction, but rather a claims-processing rule, "a precondition to filing a claim that does not restrict a federal court's subject matter jurisdiction."[19]

B. Use of Copies in Violation of Section 106: Liability for Online Service Providers

2. *Right of Distribution or Display*

   a. *Rights of Distribution and Display Implicated by Electronic Bulletin Board Services*

[Add the following text at the end of the section.]

Subsequent cases have called into question the holding of direct infringement in *Arista Records*.[20] In *Disney Enterprises, Inc. v. Hotfile Corp.*,[21] Disney sued Hotfile Corp., a Panamanian Web site operator, for direct and secondary copyright infringement. The court found that the defendants were not liable for direct infringement merely because they allowed others to upload and download copyrightable material through their Web site. The court specifically rejected the holding in *Arista Records* that a policy of encouraging infringement coupled with the ability—but refusal—to stop the infringement was a "volitional act" giving rise to direct infringement liability. The court held that this holding ignored the *Netcom* line of cases that "'knowledge coupled with inducement'" or "'supervision coupled with a financial interest in the illegal copying' gives rise to secondary infringement liability, not direct-infringement liability."[22]

---

[18] Reed Elsevier, Inc. v. Muchnick, 130 S. Ct. 1237, 176 L. Ed. 2d 18, 93 USPQ2d 1719 (2010).

[19] *Id.* at 1241, 176 L. Ed. 2d at 24.

[20] Arista Records LLC v. Usenet.com, 633 F. Supp. 2d 124, 91 USPQ2d 1744 (S.D.N.Y. 2009).

[21] 798 F. Supp. 2d 1303, 100 USPQ2d 1723 (S.D. Fla. 2011).

[22] *Id.* at 1309, 100 USPQ2d at 1727 (quoting CoStar Group, Inc. v. LoopNet, Inc., 373 F.3d 544, 549, 71 USPQ2d 1096, 1100 (4th Cir. 2004)).

[Add the following new section.]

E. BitTorrent [New Topic]

A drawback to the peer-to-peer technologies at issue in the *Napster* and *Grokster* cases was that the ability to download a file is limited by the sender's upload speed and the time the parties remain online. Large files took a long time to download. This became a problem if the peer went off-line for the night. Not only did the download stop, but unless the downloader found the same peer the next day, the download had to start over from the beginning.

To solve these problems, a new type of file sharing software called Bit Torrent was developed. BitTorrent solves the large file-size problem by splitting the file into many little pieces, allowing a computer to download those pieces from many different peers at once and reassembling the pieces when they have all arrived. This means that one downloader may communicate with thirty, forty, or one hundred or more senders while downloading a file. A server called a "tracker" keeps track of which computers have a particular file and tells the client which computers to send a request.

The group of senders is referred to as a "swarm" and this downloading technique is where BitTorrent gets its name: a torrent of bits sent by the swarm. (Once downloaded, that downloader automatically becomes part of the next swarm.)

With BitTorrent, even users who are rarely online or with slower uploading capability participate in direct infringement by sending smaller pieces of the file to others.

In cases involving traditional peer-to-peer technologies, copyright holders could identify and pursue significant senders or receivers of copyrighted works. With BitTorrent, there could be thousands of persons and IP addresses involved that enable the downloading and infringement of a work, making it more difficult to identify and police. Copyright holders have had to devise new strategies to pursue infringement claims involving the use of BitTorrent.

One of the challenges in pursuing an infringement claim in this context is that BitTorrent does not require users to create an account; the user is only an IP address on the Internet. Since Internet service providers (ISPs) dynamically assign IP addresses to their customers, the changing IP address of any user further complicates the process of tracking down the actual infringers. ISPs only retain the information linking a customer to an IP address for about two months, after which the customer can no longer be linked to a particular IP address or act of infringement.

To address this problem, copyright holders have filed copyright infringement lawsuits in federal district court by suing thousands of "Doe" defendants and then seeking expedited discovery from ISPs for information on the identity of the user assigned to the IP addresses in question.[23] Because of the short data retention policies of ISPs, the plaintiffs have

---

[23] *See generally* Voltage Pictures, LLC v. Does 1-5,000, 818 F. Supp. 2d 28 (D.D.C. 2011); Patrick Collins, Inc. v. Does 1-2,590, 2011 WL 4407112 (E.D. Pa. 2012).

sought and have received expedited discovery orders for the issuance of subpoenas to ISPs to obtain this identifying information. ISPs have resisted these discovery requests as time-consuming and costly for the ISP. In several cases, Time-Warner (an ISP) attempted to limit discovery to 28 IP addresses a month.[24]

Doe defendants have also attempted to quash discovery on several grounds, the most common being: (1) lack of personal jurisdiction, (2) the First Amendment's right of anonymity, and (3) improper joinder. Each of these arguments have been mostly dismissed by the courts as premature during the expedited discovery stage of litigation. Most courts have allowed personal jurisdiction at the initial discovery stage. For example, one district court held that "[a]nalysis of personal jurisdiction is premature when Plaintiff has not identified and named the Defendants against whom claims in fact will be asserted."[25] Yet, defendants have been successful enough in arguing that tools such as reverse DNS lookup would increase the likelihood of proper personal jurisdiction that more recent suits have been more narrowly tailored in the number of Doe defendants named.[26]

In addressing whether release of identifying information should be prohibited under First Amendment principles, most courts have adopted the test set forth in *Sony Music Entertainment, Inc. v. Does 1-40*,[27] a case which involved illegal MP3 downloads. The *Sony* test calls for the court to assess whether the plaintiff's need for identifying information outweighs the putative defendants' right to First Amendment anonymity. The factors listed by the court are: "(1) a concrete showing of a prima facie claim of actionable harm; (2) specificity of the discovery request; (3) the absence of alternative means to obtain the subpoenaed information; (4) a central need for the subpoenaed information to advance the claim; and (5) the party's expectation of privacy."[28]

In a number of cases, courts have found that application of the *Sony* test does not preclude the taking of discovery.[29] As to the first factor, courts have found that plaintiffs are able to demonstrate a prima facie claim of copyright infringement against the putative defendants. The specificity requirement is usually met by narrowly tailoring the discovery to seek such identifying information as the putative defendant's name, address, telephone number, and email address. There is usually no alternative method of getting the personally identifiable information about the Doe,

---

[24] *See, e.g.,* Call of the Wild Movie, LLC v. Does 1-1,062, 770 F. Supp. 2d 332, 354 (D.D.C. 2011).

[25] West Coast Prods., Inc. v. Does 1-351, No. 4:12-cv-00504, 2012 WL 2577551, 2012 U.S. Dist. LEXIS 92239, at *11 (S.D. Tex. July 3, 2012); *see also Call of the Wild Movie,* 770 F. Supp. 2d at 345–50.

[26] *See generally* Hard Drive Prods. v. Does 1-48, No. 11 CV 9062, 2012 WL 2196038, 2012 U.S. Dist. LEXIS 82927 (N.D. Ill. June 14, 2012); Third Degree Films v. Does 1-36, No. 11-cv-15200, 2012 WL 2522151, 2012 U.S. Dist. LEXIS 87891 (E.D. Mich. May 29, 2012); First Time Videos, LLC v. Does 1-76, 276 F.R.D. 254, 258, 2011 U.S. Dist. LEXIS 91230, at *12, 101 USPQ2d 1543, 1456 (N.D. Ill. Aug. 16, 2011).

[27] Sony Music Entm't, Inc. v. Does 1-40, 326 F. Supp. 2d 556, 71 USPQ2d 1661 (S.D.N.Y. 2004).

[28] *Id.* at 564–65, 71 USPQ2d at 1667 (citing cases for each of these factors).

[29] *Call of the Wild Movie,* 770 F. Supp. 2d at 351–53.

meaning the claim could otherwise not be advanced because the Doe could not be served. And finally, ISP privacy policies taking advantage of the protections of the DCMA typically state that subscriber information will be released in response to legal actions alleging illegal activity, meaning subscribers cannot have an expectation of privacy for illegal acts.[30]

Courts have split on the permissive joinder argument. Rule 20 of the Federal Rules of Civil Procedure permits joinder if (1) "any right to relief is asserted against [the joined defendants] jointly, severally, or in the alternative with respect to or arising out of the same transaction, occurrence, or series of transactions or occurrences"[31] and (2) "any question of law or fact common to all defendants will arise in the action."[32] In *West Coast Productions, Inc. v. Does 1-351*,[33] the United States District Court for the Southern District of Texas found that both prongs of the permissive joinder requirements were met. The court first noted that the alleged Bit-Torrent activity arose out of the same transaction and occurrence—i.e., numerous defendants participating in a concerted action to reproduce and distribute the plaintiff's video through the swarm.[34] The court also found there were various common questions of law and fact to justify permissive joinder, i.e., the court needed "to determine whether copying has occurred within the meaning of the Copyright Act, whether entering and/or remaining in a torrent swarm constitutes a willful act of infringement or civil conspiracy, and whether and to what extent Plaintiff has been damaged by one or more Defendants' conduct."[35]

Other courts have reached a different conclusion. For example, in *Patrick Collins, Inc. v. Does 1-8*,[36] the United States District Court for the Eastern District of Pennsylvania found that the fact that the plaintiff had not sufficiently alleged that the defendants had participated in the same transaction or occurrence. The court noted that the "[m]ere fact that any of the Doe Defendants may have allegedly clicked on a command to participate in the internet file sharing does not mean that each, together, was part of the downloading done by hundreds or thousands of individuals."[37] The court particularly noted that the allegations involved activities occurred over the course of seven-week period. The court found that in these circumstances that permitting joinder was not only impracticable, but would undermine Rule 20(a)'s purpose of promoting judicial efficiency, would "go against notions of fundamental fairness," and would "ultimately cause prejudice to defendants."[38]

---

[30] *Id.*

[31] FED. R. CIV. P. 20(a)(2)(A).

[32] *Id.* 20(a)(2)(B).

[33] No. 4:12-cv-00504, 2012 WL 2577551, 2012 U.S. Dist. LEXIS 92239 (S.D. Tex. July 3, 2012).

[34] *West Coast Productions, Inc. v. Does 1-351*, 2012 WL 2577551 (S.D. Tex. July 3, 2012), 2012 U.S. Dist. LEXIS 92239, at *7–8.

[35] *Id.*, 2012 U.S. Dist. LEXIS 92239, at *8–9.

[36] Patrick Collins, Inc. v. Does 1-18, No. 2:11-cv-07252, 2012 WL 1686071 (E.D. Pa. Mar. 8, 2012).

[37] *Id.*

[38] *Id.* N.D. Cal. *See also* Hard Drive Prods., Inc. v. Does 1-188, 809 F. Supp. 2d 1150, 1164 (N.D. Ca. 2011).

5

The Digital Millennium Copyright Act and Its Effect on Copyright Owners and Service Providers Online

Joshua L. Simmons
Kirkland & Ellis LLP
New York, New York

II. Impact of the DMCA in Protecting Copyright Owners' Rights Online

A. Circumvention of Copyright Protection

2. *The Extent of Section 1201: Case Law Interpretation*

a. *What Constitutes "Circumvention of a Technological Copyright Protection Measure"?*

iii. Other Copyright Circumvention Techniques

[Add the following text after the first paragraph on page 215.]

On appeal, the Ninth Circuit reversed the district court's decision except as to liability for violation of the DMCA and remanded the case.[1] The

---

[1] MDY Indus., LLC v. Blizzard Entm't, Inc., 629 F.3d 928, 958, 97 USPQ2d 1001, 1022 (9th Cir. 2010), *as amended on denial of reh'g* (Feb. 17, 2011), *opinion amended and superseded on denial of reh'g*, No. 09-15932, 2011 WL 538748, 2011 U.S. App. LEXIS 3428 (9th Cir. Feb. 17, 2011).

court held that MDY was liable under the DMCA only for violation of Section 1201(a)(2) with respect to WoW's dynamic non-literal elements. With respect to Blizzard's Section 1201(a)(2) claims, the Ninth Circuit agreed with the district court's determination that Warden does not effectively control access to WoW's literal and individual non-literal elements but that Warden does effectively control access to WoW's dynamic non-literal elements.[2] First, WoW's literal elements are available on a user's computer once the software is installed.[3] Second, while Warden blocks access to these elements when connected to a WoW server, it does not prevent a user from accessing these elements directly from a user's computer.[4] Accordingly, the Ninth Circuit determined that "Warden is not an effective access control measure with respect to WoW's literal elements and individual non-literal elements, and therefore, that MDY does not violate §1201(a)(2) with respect to these elements."[5]

As to the dynamic non-literal elements, first, by selling Glider, the Ninth Circuit determined that the first two elements of Blizzard's Section 1201(a)(2) claim were met.[6] The next two elements were found to be satisfied because MDY marketed Glider to be used in circumventing Warden.[7] Also, there was no question that WoW's dynamic non-literal elements constituted a copyrighted work.[8] Finally, the court determined that Warden is an "effective access control measure," because in order to access Blizzard's servers, WoW's program must scan a user's computer RAM and confirm the absence of any bots or cheats.[9] Accordingly, the Ninth Circuit determined that "Warden effectively controls access to WoW's dynamic non-literal elements," and thus "MDY is liable under §1201(a)(2) with respect to WoW's dynamic non-literal elements."[10]

The Ninth Circuit concluded, however, that "Warden does not effectively protect any of Blizzard's rights under the Copyright Act, and MDY is not liable under §1201(b)(1) for Glider's circumvention of Warden."[11] First, the court found that although Blizzard's contract with its users prohibited the use of software such as Glider, the prohibition was a covenant, not a condition, which meant that even if users violated the covenant by using Glider, they do not infringe Blizzard's copyrights by doing so.[12] Second, there was no evidence that Warden detected or prevented users from recording game play by taking screenshots.[13]

[Add the following text at the end of the section.]

---

[2] *Id.* at 952–54, 97 USPQ2d at 1017–19.
[3] *Id.* at 952, 97 USPQ2d at 1017.
[4] *Id.* at 953, 97 USPQ2d at 1018.
[5] *Id.*, 97 USPQ2d at 1018.
[6] *Id.*, 97 USPQ2d at 1018.
[7] *Id.*, 97 USPQ2d at 1018.
[8] *Id.*, 97 USPQ2d at 1018.
[9] *Id.* at 954, 97 USPQ2d at 1019.
[10] *Id.*, 97 USPQ2d at 1019.
[11] *Id.* at 955, 97 USPQ2d at 1019.
[12] *Id.* at 954, 97 USPQ2d at 1019.
[13] *Id.* 954–55, 97 USPQ2d at 1019.

In *TracFone Wireless, Inc. v. Technopark Co.,*[14] the plaintiff marketed prepaid cell phones that were to be used only on the plaintiff's wireless network. TracFone accused Technopark of selling hardware and software that circumvented the plaintiff's copyrighted and proprietary software by reflashing and unlocking the TracFone phones, which allowed the phones to be used on wireless networks other than TracFone network.[15] The defendant failed to respond to the plaintiff's complaint, and the court determined that, as alleged, the defendant's unlocking technology constituted a circumvention measure prohibited by the statute and entered judgment against the defendant.[16]

> iv.   What Does NOT Constitute Circumvention of Technological Copyright Protection Measures

[Add the following new text at the end of the section.]

The Fifth Circuit withdrew its prior opinion in *MGE UPS Systems, Inc. v. GE Consumer & Industrial, Inc.*[17] after granting rehearing in part. In any case, in the substituted opinion the Fifth Circuit again held that MGE failed to prove GE circumvented the technology, because "MGE did not present any evidence showing that a GE/PMI representative altered the Pacret and Muguet software such that a dongle was not required to use the software; rather, employees simply used the software after the alteration was made."[18]

> c.   *Exemptions*

[Add the following text at the end of the section.]

At the time of this writing, the Copyright Office is conducting a rulemaking to designate the classes of works that will be exempt from the prohibitions against circumvention of technological measures that control access to copyrighted works when such circumvention is done to engage in non-infringing uses of works in the designated classes. In its December 20, 2011 Notice of Proposed Rulemaking, the Copyright Office identified the following classes of works, which were proposed by various parties during the comment period:

---

[14]No. 12 Civ. 20013, 2012 WL 1229454, 2012 U.S. Dist. LEXIS 58449 (S.D. Fla. Apr. 9, 2012).

[15]*Id.* at *1, 2012 U.S. Dist. LEXIS 58449, at *3–4.

[16]*Id.* at *5, 2012 U.S. Dist. LEXIS 58449, at *9–10; *see also* Dish Network L.L.C. v. Rounds, No. 11 Civ. 241, 2012 WL 1158798, 2012 U.S. Dist. LEXIS 48892 (W.D. Pa. Apr. 6, 2012) (entering default judgment based on the defendant's providing technology that decrypted the plaintiff's encrypted satellite signal into viewable programming that could be displayed on a television without payment to the plaintiff).

[17]*See* 612 F.3d 760, 95 USPQ2d 1632 (5th Cir.), *withdrawn, reh'g in part granted and opinion substituted*, 622 F.3d 361, 96 USPQ2d 1123 (5th Cir. 2010).

[18]*Id.* at 366, 96 USPQ2d at 1126.

1. Literary works in the public domain that are made available in digital copies.

2. Literary works, distributed electronically, that: (1) Contain digital rights management and/or other access controls which either prevent the enabling of the book's read-aloud functionality or which interfere with screen readers or other applications or assistive technologies that render the text in specialized formats; and (2) are legally obtained by blind or other persons with print disabilities (as such persons are defined in section 121 of Title 17, United States Code), or are legally obtained by authorized entities (as defined in such section) distributing such work exclusively to such persons.

3. Computer programs that enable lawfully acquired video game consoles to execute lawfully acquired software applications, where circumvention is undertaken for the purpose of enabling interoperability of such applications with computer programs on the gaming console.

4. Computer programs that enable the installation and execution of lawfully obtained software on a personal computing device, where circumvention is performed by or at the request of the device's owner.

5. Computer programs that enable wireless telephone handsets ("smartphones") and tablets to execute lawfully obtained software applications, where circumvention is undertaken for the purpose of enabling interoperability of such applications with computer programs on the handset or tablet.

6A. Computer programs, in the form of firmware or software, including data used by those programs, that enable mobile devices to connect to a wireless communications network, when circumvention is initiated by the owner of the device to remove a restriction that limits the device's operability to a limited number of networks, or circumvention is initiated to connect to a wireless communications network.

6B. Computer programs, in the form of firmware or software, including data used by those programs, that enable wireless devices to connect to a wireless communications network, when circumvention is initiated by the owner of the copy of the computer program principally in order to connect to a wireless communications network and access to such communications network is authorized by the operator of such communications network.

6C. Computer programs, in the form of firmware or software, including data used by those programs, that enable wireless devices to connect to a wireless communications network, when circumvention is initiated by the owner of the copy of the computer program solely in order to connect to a wireless communications network and access to such communications network is authorized by the operator of such communications network.

7A. Motion pictures on DVDs that are lawfully made and acquired and that are protected by the Content Scrambling System when circumvention is accomplished solely in order to accomplish the incorporation of short portions of motion pictures into new works for the purpose of criticism or comment, and where the person engaging in circumvention believes and has reasonable grounds for believing that circumvention is necessary to fulfill the purpose of the use in the following instances: (i) Educational uses by college and university professors and by college and university film and media studies students; (ii) Documentary filmmaking; (iii) Noncommercial videos.

7B. Audiovisual works on DVDs that are lawfully made and acquired and that are protected by the Content Scrambling System, where circumvention is undertaken for the purpose of extracting clips for inclusion in primarily noncommercial videos that do not infringe copyright, and the person engaging in the circumvention believes and has reasonable grounds for believing that circumvention is necessary to fulfill the purpose of the use.

7C. Audiovisual works that are lawfully made and acquired via online distribution services, where circumvention is undertaken for the purpose of extracting clips for inclusion in primarily noncommercial videos that do not infringe copyright, and the person engaging in the circumvention believes and has reasonable grounds for believing that circumvention is necessary to fulfill the purpose of the use, and the works in question are not readily available on DVD.

7D. Motion pictures that are lawfully made and acquired from DVDs protected by the Content Scrambling System and Blu-Ray discs protected by Advanced Access Content System, or, if the motion picture is not reasonably available on DVD or Blu-Ray or not reasonably available in sufficient audiovisual quality on DVD or Blu-Ray, then from digitally transmitted video protected by an authentication protocol or by encryption, when circumvention is accomplished solely in order to incorporate short portions of motion pictures into new works for the purpose of fair use, and when the person engaging in circumvention reasonably believes that circumvention is necessary to obtain the motion picture in the following instances: (1) Documentary filmmaking; OR (2) fictional filmmaking.

7E. Motion pictures that are lawfully made and acquired from DVDs protected by the Content Scrambling System or, if the motion picture is not reasonably available on or not reasonably available in sufficient audiovisual quality on DVD, then from digitally transmitted video protected by an authentication protocol or by encryption, when circumvention is accomplished solely in order to incorporate short portions of motion pictures into new works for the purpose of fair use, and when the person engaging in circumvention reasonably believes that circumvention is necessary to obtain the motion picture for multimedia e-book authorship.

7F. Motion pictures on DVDs that are lawfully made and acquired and that are protected by the Content Scrambling System when circumvention is accomplished solely in order to accomplish the incorporation of short portions of motion pictures into new works for the purpose of criticism or comment, and where the person engaging in circumvention believes and has reasonable grounds for believing that circumvention is necessary to fulfill the purpose of educational uses by college and university professors and by college and university film and media studies students.

7G. Audiovisual works (optical discs, streaming media, and downloads) that are lawfully made and acquired when circumvention is accomplished by college and university students or faculty (including teaching and research assistants) solely in order to incorporate short portions of video into new works for the purpose of criticism or comment.

8.   Lawfully accessed audiovisual works used for educational purposes by kindergarten through twelfth grade educators.

9A. Motion pictures and other audiovisual works delivered via Internet protocol (IP) protected by technological measures that control access to such works when circumvention is accomplished to facilitate the creation, improvement, or rendering of visual representations or descriptions of audible portions of such works for the purpose of improving the ability of individuals who may lawfully access such works to perceive such works.

9B. Motion pictures and other audiovisual works delivered via Internet protocol (IP) protected by technological measures that control access to such works when circumvention is accomplished to facilitate the creation, improvement, or rendering of audible representations or descriptions of visual portions of such works for the purpose of improving the ability of individuals who may lawfully access such works to perceive such works.

9C. Motion pictures and other audiovisual works on fixed disc-based media protected by technological measures that control access to such works when circumvention is accomplished to facilitate the creation, improvement, or rendering of visual representations or descriptions of audible portions of such works for the purpose of improving the ability of individuals who may lawfully access such works to perceive such works.

9D. Motion pictures and other audiovisual works on fixed disc-based media protected by technological measures that control access to such works when circumvention is accomplished to facilitate the creation, improvement, or rendering of audible representations or descriptions of visual portions of such works for the purpose of improving the ability of individuals who may lawfully access such works to perceive such works.

10A. Motion pictures on lawfully made and lawfully acquired DVDs that are protected by the Content Scrambling System when circumvention is accomplished solely in order to accomplish the noncommercial space shifting of the contained motion picture.

10B. Legally acquired digital media (motion pictures, sound recordings, and e-books) for personal use and for the purposes of making back-up copies, format shifting, access, and transfer.[19]

B. Falsification of Copyright Management Information

2. What Is "Copyright Management Information"?: Disagreement Among Circuits

[132a][Add new footnote following the word "reversed" in the last line of the first paragraph on page 225.] Murphy v. Millennium Radio Group LLC, 650 F.3d 295, 99 USPQ2d 1022 (3d Cir. 2011).

[134][Add to footnote 134 on page 226.] See also Hanover Architectural Serv., P.A. v. Christian Testimony-Morris, N.P., No. 10 Civ. 5455, 2011 WL 6002045, at *7, 2011 U.S. Dist. LEXIS 137201, at *20–21 (D.N.J. Nov. 29,

---

[19]Exemption to Prohibition on Circumvention of Copyright Protection Systems for Access Control Technologies, 76 Fed. Reg. 78,866 (Dec. 15, 2011) (to be codified at 37 C.F.R. pt. 201), available at http://www.copyright.gov/fedreg/2011/76fr78866.pdf. Proponents of each proposed rule are listed following the rule.

2011) (rejecting the defendant's argument that CMI must function as a component of an automated copyright protection or management system based on the Third Circuit's decision in *Murphy v. Millennium Radio Group LLC*).

[Add the following text at the end of the section.]

In *Personal Keepsakes, Inc. v. PersonalizationMall.com, Inc.*,[20] the operator of a Web site selling "personalized gifts and knickknacks" sued a group of defendants who sold similar products, alleging that they took the plaintiff's copyrighted poems and incorporated them into their own products.[21] In support of its Section 1202 claim, the plaintiff asserted "(1) that Defendants removed the CMI conveyed with the poems when it copied the poems, and (2) Defendants provided false CMI on the pages selling the infringing products and in their general website terms and conditions, which make various statements about copyrights on the website."[22]

As to the first allegation, the plaintiff asserted three pieces of purported CMI had been removed when the defendants copied its poems: its Web site name, the titles of the works, and the copyright notice on the bottom of each Web page.[23] The court, however, determined that none of these items constituted CMI. First, the Web site name—poetrygift.com—and the titles of the works—"Baptism Gifts"/"On Your Baptism Day" and "Ring Bearer Gift"/"To Our Ring Bearer"—did not equate to the copyright owner—PKI—or titles of the works—"Personal Keepsakes VI" and "Personal Keepsakes X"—in the plaintiff's copyright registrations.[24] The court concluded that because "the point of CMI is to inform the public that something is copyrighted and to prevent infringement," a DMCA claim predicated on alleged CMI "that does not link up in any way to the copyright registration" does not state a claim under the statute.[25] Second, the court determined that because the exhibits to the plaintiff's complaint did not show any copyright notices were used in connection with the plaintiff's works, the plaintiff could not state a claim based on the notices.[26]

As to the second allegation, the court found that the plaintiff did state a Section 1202 claim based on one defendant's use of a copyright notice that could plausibly refer to the poem on its product, which was identical to the plaintiff's copyrighted poem.[27] The plaintiff also alleged

---

[20] No. 11 Civ. 5177, 2012 WL 414803, 2012 U.S. Dist. LEXIS 15280, 101 USPQ2d 1855 (N.D. Ill. Feb. 8, 2012).

[21] *Id.* at *1, 2012 U.S. Dist. LEXIS 15280, at *1–2, 101 USPQ2d at 1856–57.

[22] *Id.* at *6, 2012 U.S. Dist. LEXIS 15280, at *17, 101 USPQ2d at 1862.

[23] *Id.* at *6, 2012 U.S. Dist. LEXIS 15280, at *18, 101 USPQ2d at 1862.

[24] *Id.* at *6, 2012 U.S. Dist. LEXIS 15280, at *18, 101 USPQ2d at 1862.

[25] *Id.* at *6, 2012 U.S. Dist. LEXIS 15280, at *18–19, 101 USPQ2d at 1862.

[26] *Id.* at *6, 2012 U.S. Dist. LEXIS 15280, at *19, 101 USPQ2d at 1862.

[27] *Id.* at *7, 2012 U.S. Dist. LEXIS 15280, at *20–21, 101 USPQ2d at 1862–63. As the other defendants did not include a copyright notice with their use of the poem, the court held that the plaintiff did not state a claim as to them. *Id.* at *7, 2012 U.S. Dist. LEXIS 15280, at *21–22, 101 USPQ2d at 1863.

that because the defendants made statements in their Web sites' terms and conditions pages that all of their Web sites' content was owned by them, they violated Section 1202. The court, however, concluded that CMI is not "conveyed" with a work when it appears in a general copyright notice on an entirely different Web page, and thus a DMCA claim based thereon would not lie.[28]

C. Civil Remedies and Criminal Penalties Under the DMCA

[Add the following text at the end of the carry-over paragraph on page 228.]

Courts have also elected to reduce a plaintiff's statutory damages award under Section 1203 where a reduced award serves as a deterrent.[29]

IV. INTERNET SERVICE PROVIDER LIABILITY

B. Types of Actions on Part of an ISP Subject to Limited Liability

3. *Information Stored at the Direction of the User*

[Add the following text after the first full paragraph on page 242.]

The Ninth Circuit affirmed the district court opinion on appeal.[30] First, the court determined that Section 512(c) "encompasses the access-facilitating processes that automatically occur when a user uploads a video to Veoh."[31] Second, the court found that the district court had properly determined that Veoh did not have knowledge or awareness of infringing videos that it did not remove.[32] In particular, the court noted that because music videos could legally appear on Veoh, it could not be held to have the requisite knowledge necessarily to support UMG's claim based solely on a general knowledge that its services could be used to post infringing

---

[28] *Id.* at *7, 2012 U.S. Dist. LEXIS 15280, at *22, 101 USPQ2d at 1863.

[29] *See Nexon Am. Inc. v. Kumar*, No. 2:11 Civ. 6991, 2012 WL 1116328, at *7, 2012 U.S. Dist. LEXIS 47294, at *20 (C.D. Cal. Apr. 3, 2012) (refusing to grant statutory maximum award of $44,845,000, but rather granting statutory minimum award of $3,587,600). The court considered "even the minimum statutory amount awardable under the DMCA in this case to be a significant windfall to Plaintiff far in excess of any amount necessary to deter future infringing conduct. Further, the minimum award here likely bears little plausible relationship to Plaintiff's actual damages. Nevertheless, the Court is powerless the deviate from the DMCA's statutory minimum." *Id.* at *7, 2012 U.S. Dist. LEXIS 47294, at *20.

[30] UMG Recordings, Inc. v. Shelter Capital Partners LLC, 667 F.3d 1022, 1031, 101 USPQ2d 1001, 1006 (9th Cir. 2011).

[31] *Id.* at 1031, 101 USPQ2d at 1007.

[32] *Id.* at 1036, 101 USPQ2d at 1010.

material.[33] Similarly, the court discounted Veoh's other "purported evidence of Veoh's actual or apparent knowledge of infringement."[34] Finally, the court agreed with the district court's finding that Veoh did not have the necessary right and ability to control infringing activity to prevent it from taking advantage of the safe harbor.[35] The court noted that "a service provider may, as a general matter, have the legal right and necessary technology to remove infringing content, but until it becomes aware of specific unauthorized material, it cannot exercise its 'power or authority' over the specific infringing item."[36] Accordingly, UMG did not have the requisite ability to control infringing activity contemplated by the statute.[37]

[Add the following text after the first paragraph on page 243.]

On appeal, the Second Circuit vacated the district court's order, because it determined that "a reasonable jury could conclude that YouTube had knowledge or awareness under §512(c)(1)(A) at least with respect to a handful of specific clips."[38] The court recognized that Section 512(c) requires knowledge or awareness of specific infringing activities.[39] Moreover, it clarified that the difference between "actual" and "red flag" knowledge under the statute is between "subjective" and "objective" knowledge, and not between "specific" and "generalized" knowledge.[40] Nevertheless, the court determined that the district court's grant of summary judgment was premature as the plaintiffs may have raised "material issues of fact regarding YouTube's knowledge or 'red flag' awareness of specific instances of infringement."[41]

The Second Circuit also determined that the willful blindness doctrine "may be applied, in appropriate circumstances, to demonstrate knowledge or awareness of specific instances of infringement under §512(c)(1)(A)."[42] The court found that a person is "willfully blind" or engages in "conscious avoidance" amounting to knowledge where the person is "aware of a high probability of the fact in dispute and consciously avoided confirming that fact."[43] Accordingly, the court remanded to the district court to determine whether the defendants made a deliberate effort to avoid guilty knowledge of infringement.[44]

The Second Circuit further determined that the district court had erred "by requiring 'item-specific' knowledge of infringement in its

---

[33] *Id.* at 1036–38, 101 USPQ2d at 1011–12.

[34] *Id.* at 1038, 101 USPQ2d at 1012–13.

[35] *Id.* at 1041, 101 USPQ2d at 1014–15.

[36] *Id.*, 101 USPQ2d at 1015.

[37] *Id.* at 1041–43, 101 USPQ2d at 1015–16.

[38] Viacom Int'l, Inc. v. YouTube, Inc., 676 F.3d 19, 41, 102 USPQ2d 1283, 1296 (2d Cir. 2012).

[39] *Id.* at 30, 102 USPQ2d at 1288.

[40] *Id.* at 31, 102 USPQ2d at 1289.

[41] *Id.* at 32–34, 102 USPQ2d at 1290–91.

[42] *Id.* at 41, 102 USPQ2d at 1296.

[43] *Id.* at 35, 102 USPQ2d at 1291 (quoting United States v. Aina-Marshall, 336 F.3d 167, 170 (2d Cir. 2003)).

[44] *Id.* at 35, 102 USPQ2d at 1292.

interpretation of the 'right and ability to control' infringing activity under 17 U.S.C. §512(c)(1)(B)."[45] Instead, the court concluded that a defendant must have "more than the ability to remove or block access to materials posted on a service provider's website," but did not determine the "more difficult" question of what that "something more" required.[46]

Finally, the Second Circuit held that the district court held correctly that "three of the challenged YouTube software functions—replication, playback, and the related videos feature—occur 'by reason of the storage at the direction of a user' within the meaning of 17 U.S.C. §512(c)(1)."[47] The court, however, remanded for "further fact-finding with respect to a fourth software function, involving the third-party syndication of videos uploaded to YouTube."[48]

In a similar Second Circuit case, the Southern District of New York held that Photobucket could not be held liable for infringing the plaintiff's work because it fell within the Section 512(c) safe harbor.[49] Photobucket is a photo-sharing ISP that operates a Web site that allows users to upload content to be stored or viewed on its Web site.[50] Photobucket does not charge its users to use its Web site, instead receiving the majority of its income from advertising revenue.[51]

First, the court determined that Photobucket satisfies the threshold requirements to qualify for the safe harbor. Photobucket meets the DM-CA's definition of a service provider, because, like YouTube and Veoh, it hosts users' content and allows them to share that content at their own direction.[52] Photobucket also adopted and reasonably implemented a policy for the termination in appropriate circumstances of users who are repeat infringers, as it has a take-down policy and when it received the plaintiff's take-down notices, it acted to remove the infringing material.[53] The plaintiff alleged that Photobucket did not meet the third threshold requirement as it "accommodates and does not interfere with standard technical measures" used by copyright owners to identify or protect copyrighted works because it provided photo-editing tools that "allow[ed] users to obliterate, hide or crop out the copyright watermarks on the electronic images uploaded" to its Web site.[54] The court, however, found no evidence that Photobucket advised or encouraged users to use the tools for that purpose—rather, watermarks did appear on the Photobucket Web site, suggesting that it did accommodate such measures.[55]

---

[45] Id. at 42, 102 USPQ2d at 1297.
[46] Id. at 38, 102 USPQ2d at 1294.
[47] Id. at 42, 102 USPQ2d at 1297.
[48] Id. at 39, 102 USPQ2d at 1294.
[49] Wolk v. Kodak Imaging Network, Inc., 840 F. Supp. 2d 724, 743, 102 USPQ2d 1652 (S.D.N.Y. 2012).
[50] Id. at 730.
[51] Id.
[52] Id. at 743–44.
[53] Id. at 744.
[54] Id. at 744–45.
[55] Id. at 745.

Second, the court held that Photobucket did not have actual knowledge of infringing activity and that it was not aware of any fact from which infringing activity was apparent.[56] There was no evidence that Photobucket had "actual or constructive knowledge" of the plaintiff's alleged copyright infringement.[57] In addition, the court found that the eleven of the plaintiff's take-down notices were not DMCA-compliant, and thus did not provide Photobucket with constructive knowledge of the infringement.[58] Moreover, although the plaintiff alleged that one notice of infringement should be sufficient to apply to all instances of that image appearing on Photobucket's Web site, the court held that "[n]otices that do not identify the specific location of the alleged infringement are not sufficient to confer 'actual knowledge' on the service provider."[59] Where the plaintiff did provide Photobucket with DMCA-compliant notices, the evidence showed that Photobucket expeditiously took down the infringing material.[60]

Third, the court held that Photobucket did not have the right and ability to control the infringements and did not receive a direct financial benefit from them. The court determined that to have the right and ability to control infringements, Photobucket would have needed to pre-screen users' content, which it did not do.[61] The court also found that Photobucket did not attract or retain subscriptions based on the infringement—rather, it found Photobucket's profits were derived from the service it provided, not a particular infringement.[62]

Finally, the court concluded that Photobucket complied with the remaining DMCA requirements, including removing content expeditiously and registering a DMCA agent with the Copyright Office.[63]

V. Remedial Steps Available to Copyright Owners, Alleged Infringers and ISPs

A. Subpoena

[Add the following text at the end of the section.]

Courts have held that a subpoena to obtain identifying information may not be directed at past infringement.[64] Rather, the subpoena power

---

[56] Id. at 746.

[57] Id.

[58] Id. at 746–47.

[59] Id. at 747. The court found to hold otherwise could result in the unlawful blocking of others from uploading images to which they hold valid licenses. Id.

[60] Id.

[61] Id. at 748.

[62] Id.

[63] Id. at 748–49.

[64] See, e.g., Maximized Living, Inc. v. Google, Inc., No. 11 Civ. 80061, 2011 WL 6749017, at *5, 2011 U.S. Dist. LEXIS 147486, at *13 (N.D. Cal. Dec. 22, 2011).

is limited to "currently infringing activity and does not reach former infringing activity that has ceased and thus can no longer be removed or disabled."[65]

Subpoenas may also issue in the ordinary course of litigation pursuant to Federal Rule of Civil Procedure 45. In at least one instance, however, subpoenas seeking identifying information of non-party users was not permitted, because the identity of these individuals would not be relevant to the plaintiff's claims.[66]

---

[65] *Id.* at *6, 2011 U.S. Dist. LEXIS 147486, at *16.

[66] *See* Pacific Century Int'l, Ltd. v. Does 1-37, No. 12 Civ. 1057, 2012 WL 1072312, at *4–5, 2012 U.S. Dist. LEXIS 44368, at *13–16, 102 USPQ2d 1201, 1204–05 (N.D. Ill. Mar. 30, 2012) (refusing to compel disclosure of identifying information associated with non-party IP addresses). The Court in *Pacific Century* did, however, order the ISP to disclose the defendant's identity. *Id.* at *6, 2012 U.S. Dist. LEXIS 44368, at *19, 102 USPQ2d at 1206.

6

What May Be Protected by Copyright: Unique and Specific Applications of Copyright Law Online

Brittany Adkins Schaffer
Loeb & Loeb, LLP
Nashville, Tennessee

I. Text

A. Text Originally Created for Physical Distribution

2. *Disputes Between Copyright Owners and Third-Party Online Companies*

[Add the following text at the end of the section.]

Since Judge Chin and the U.S. District Court for the South District of New York rejected the settlement agreement between the parties in *Authors Guild v. Google, Inc.*,[1] the parties have been unable to reach a new settlement agreement and the dispute continues in court. Most recently, Google filed a motion to deny the authors' rights to proceed as a class, claiming the plaintiffs lacked associational standing. Authors Guild also filed a motion for class certification in order to proceed with its claims against the tech giant on behalf of its members.[2]

In order for Authors Guild to overcome Google's motion to dismiss, Authors Guild needed to satisfy the requirements for associational standing laid out in *Hunt v. Washington State Apple Advertising Commission*:

> "[A]n association has standing to bring suit on behalf of its members when: (a) its members would otherwise have standing to sue in their own right; (b) the interests it seeks to protect are germane to the organization's purpose; and (c) neither the claim asserted nor the relief requested requires the participation of individual members in the lawsuit."[3]

Google did not dispute the first two prongs of the *Hunt* test, but argued against the third prong, claiming that participation of the organization's members was required under the circumstances. The court disagreed. Finding that application of the third prong prudential and the equities aligning in favor of associational standing, the court held that the third prong was satisfied and that Authors Guild, therefore, had standing to pursue the copyright infringement claims on behalf of its members.[4]

According to the district court, only limited individual participation of Authors Guild members would be necessary to prove the association's copyright infringement claims.[5] To establish copyright infringement, a plaintiff must prove "'(1) ownership of a valid copyright, and (2) copying of constituent elements of the work that are original.'"[6] The second element was easily satisfied, as "Google does not deny that it openly copied millions of books—original works—without the permission of the

---

[1] Authors Guild v. Google, Inc., No. 05 Civ. 8136, 10 Civ. 2977, 2012 WL 1951790, 2012 U.S. Dist. LEXIS 76080, 102 USPQ2d 1916 (S.D.N.Y. May 31, 2012).

[2] *Id.* at *2–3, 2012 U.S. Dist. LEXIS 76080, at *9, 102 USPQ2d at 1917.

[3] *Id.* at *3, 2012 U.S. Dist. LEXIS 76080, at *15–16, 102 USPQ2d at 1919 (quoting Hunt v. Washington State Apple Advertising Comm'n, 432 U.S. 333, 343 (1997)).

[4] *Id.* at *43–46, 2012 U.S. Dist. LEXIS 76080, at *16–27, 102 USPQ2d at 1919–21.

[5] *Id.*, 2012 U.S. Dist. LEXIS 76080, at *21, 102 USPQ2d at 1920.

[6] *Id.*, 2012 U.S. Dist. LEXIS 76080, at *21, 102 USPQ2d at 1920 (quoting Arista Records, LLC v. Doe 3, 604 F.3d 110, 117, 94 USPQ2d 1587, 1592 (2d Cir. 2010)).

copyright holders" and posted those snippets of those books online without permission.[7] Although slightly more challenging, proving ownership of a valid copyright requires little to no individual participation either. Copyright ownership information is publicly available through the United States Copyright Office's Registry. Because copyright registrations are *prima facie* evidence of copyright ownership, Authors Guild members who retained all or part of their copyright did not need to individually participate in the claim to prove ownership.[8] Guild members who had assigned their copyrights to third-parties, but who retained a "beneficial interest" in their works (such as receiving royalties), might have to participate in the claim individually by producing valid, legal documentation, such publishing contracts, to prove their beneficial interest in the applicable copyrighted works. However, the court found that requiring some Authors Guild members to provide documentation of their beneficial interest in the copyright would be a reasonable request and "would not make this case administratively inconvenient or unmanageable."[9] "The alternative—forcing association members to pursue their claims individually," explained the court, "would be burdensome and inefficient."[10]

The court also adamantly rejected Google's contention that two fair use factors essential to Google's defense—"the nature of the copyrighted work" and "the effect of the use upon the potential market for or value of the copyrighted work"—required an individual inquiry of each Authors Guild member and work.[11] The court explained that "[w]hile different classes of works may require different treatment for the purposes of 'fair use,' the fair-use analysis does not require individual participation of association members," and suggested that Google's contentions could be accommodated by grouping similar association members and their respective works in subgroups (i.e., photographers in one group; fiction writers in another, etc.).[12] Furthermore, the court did not hide his distaste for Google's fair use argument, stating:

> [G]iven the sweeping and undiscriminating nature of Google's unauthorized copying, it would be unjust to require that each affected association member litigate his claim individually. When Google copied works, it did not conduct an inquiry into the copyright ownership of each work; nor did it conduct an individualized evaluation as to whether posting "snippets" of a particular work would constitute "fair use." It copied and made search results available *en masse*.... Because Google treated the copyright holders as a group, the copyright holders should be able to litigate on a group basis.[13]

---

[7] *Id.*, 2012 U.S. Dist. LEXIS 76080, at *21, 102 USPQ2d at 1920.

[8] *Id.* at *5, 2012 U.S. Dist. LEXIS 76080, at *21–22, 102 USPQ2d at 1920 (referencing www.copyright.gov/records for books registered with the U.S. Copyright Office since Jan. 1, 1978).

[9] *Id.*, 2012 U.S. Dist. LEXIS 76080, at *22–23, 102 USPQ2d at 1920.

[10] *Id.*, 2012 U.S. Dist. LEXIS 76080, at *23, 102 USPQ2d at 1920.

[11] *Id.*, 2012 U.S. Dist. LEXIS 76080, at *23–24, 102 USPQ2d at 1921 (citing 17 U.S.C. §107(2), (4) (two of the four fair use factors)).

[12] *Id.*, 2012 U.S. Dist. LEXIS 76080, at *24, 102 USPQ2d at 1921.

[13] *Id.*, 2012 U.S. Dist. LEXIS 76080, at *26–27, 102 USPQ2d at 1921.

The court, therefore, found the equities weighed in favor of associational standing to proceed.

With respect to Authors Guild's motion for class certification, the court granted its motion and certified the class to proceed.[14] In coming to this conclusion, the court noted that Google did not dispute that the proposed class was satisfied procedurally under Federal Rule of Civil Procedure 23(a),[15] but argued that the adequacy requirement for class certification under that rule was not met because most class members viewed Google's copying of their work as beneficial, both financially and in terms of exposure.[16] In particular, Google cited a survey in which a few more than 500 authors (58% of the surveyed population) stated that they "approve" of Google's copying of their work for search-related purposes, and approximately 170 (19% of those surveyed) "feel" they will financially benefit either now or in the future from Google actions of scanning and making available snippets of their work.[17] The court rejected Google's arguments as without merit, finding that the lead plaintiffs adequately represented the class and that Google had "not pointed to any legal or factual argument made by the lead plaintiffs that would undermine the copyright claim of any other class member."[18] Furthermore, the court found Google's contention that some class members might not wish to pursue claims was an inadequate basis for rejecting class certification and noted that the aforementioned survey did not ask an important question—"whether they would want to be part of a law suit through which they might recover damages."[19] Finally, the court held that under Rule 23(b)(3) the common issues in this litigation predominated over any individual claims that might arise and that class action was a superior way to resolve this litigation.[20]

Despite the recent rulings, the conflict described in in *Authors Guild v. Google* will continue with the further development and use of the Internet.

II. IMAGES

B. Third-Party Display of Images Online: Thumbnail Images, Framing, and Linking

2. *Fair Use Defense*

[Add the following text at the end of the section.]

---

[14] *Id.* at *11, 2012 U.S. Dist. LEXIS 76080, at *41, 102 USPQ2d at 1925.

[15] *Id.* at *9, 2012 U.S. Dist. LEXIS 76080, at *35, 102 USPQ2d at 1924 (satisfying Rule 23(a)'s numerosity, commonality, and typicality requirements).

[16] *Id.* at *10, 2012 U.S. Dist. LEXIS 76080, at *36, 102 USPQ2d at 1924.

[17] *Id.*, 2012 U.S. Dist. LEXIS 76080, at *36, 102 USPQ2d at 1924.

[18] *Id.*, 2012 U.S. Dist. LEXIS 76080, at *36–37, 102 USPQ2d at 1924.

[19] *Id.*, 2012 U.S. Dist. LEXIS 76080, at *38, 102 USPQ2d at 1924.

[20] *Id.* at *11, 2012 U.S. Dist. LEXIS 76080, at *38–41, 102 USPQ2d at 1925.

One of the most recent debates and issues to watch with respect to images and fair use concerns the social networking Web site Pinterest, "an online and mobile service that allows you to create online pinboards and organize and share beautiful things you find on the web."[21] Essentially, Pinterest is a "virtual pinboard" that allows a user to "pin" his or her favorite images to a virtual bulletin board that other Pinterest users may view and follow. The controversy lies in the fact that users often pin copyrighted images without first obtaining permission from the copyright owners.

Pinterest seems to be formatting its Web site to suggest that the use of the pinned images is a fair use and that permission is, therefore, not essential for appropriate use of the images. Initially, the Web site asked users to "describe" the images pinned to their individual pinboards. Pinterest now encourages users to "comment" on the pin, suggesting an effort to appeal to the fair use factors—i.e., using the image for the purposes of comment and/or criticism.[22] Although a pin generally includes the entire copyrighted image, the use of the pinned image is not seemingly commercial at this time and is arguably transformative under the reasoning of *Perfect 10 Inc. v. Amazon.com, Inc.*[23] Furthermore, Pinterest's "Pin Etiquette" requests that users link each pin to its original source.[24] As with thumbnail images used in a search engine, the pin may "transform[] the image into a pointer directing a user to a source of information ... and provide[] a social benefit by incorporating an original work into a new work, namely, an electronic reference tool."[25] In this event, there is likely little to no negative effect "upon the potential market for or value of the copyrighted work."[26] In fact, the exact opposite may occur. If use of pins drives traffic to the original source of the image, it increases the likelihood that the potential market for or value of the copyrighted work will grow through the increased exposure.

No court has yet addressed this particular service. But Pinterest has implemented safeguards to protect itself in the event images uploaded infringe copyrights. To start, Pinterest has claimed protection under the safe harbor of the Digital Millennium Copyright Act of 1998. The Web site states: "It is Pinterest's policy, in appropriate circumstances and at its discretion, to disable and/or terminate the accounts of users who repeatedly infringe or are repeatedly charged with infringing the copyrights

---

[21]Pinterest, Terms & Privacy, http://pinterest.com/about/terms/ (last visited July 1, 2012).

[22]*See* 17 U.S.C. §107. However, some sources indicate that Pinterest and its investors may be exploring ways to monetize infringing pins, which could complicate a fair use argument. Deborah Sweeney, *Pinning Copyright Complaints on Pinterest*, Social Media Today, Feb. 27, 2012, http://socialmediatoday.com/node/457517. At this time, however, there is no publically available information to suggest the pinned images contain a commercial purpose.

[23]508 F.3d 1146 (9th Cir. 2007).

[24]Pinterest, Pin Etiquette, http://pinterest.com/about/etiquette/ (last visited July 1, 2012).

[25]*Perfect 10*, 508 F.3d at 1165.

[26]17 U.S.C. §107(4).

or other intellectual property rights of others."[27] The Web site goes on to provide an explanation of its removal process. Pinterest's terms of use also place the burden of ensuring non-infringing images on the users. According to the terms of use:

> Pinterest values and respects the rights of third party creators and content owners, and expects you to do the same. You therefore agree that any User Content that you post to the Service does not and will not violate any law or infringe the rights of any third party, including without limitation any Intellectual Property Rights (defined below), publicity rights or rights of privacy.... It is important that you understand that you are in the best position to know if the materials you post are legally allowed.[28]

Users must also agree that, in the event Pinterest incurs any damages, costs or expenses as a result of a user's content or a breach of the terms of use, the user will "indemnify and hold harmless" Pinterest.[29] Many of these precautions will be unnecessary as it relates to copyright infringement if pinning images to this virtual bulletin board is fair use. However, until a court makes a determination or until enough time passes without incident that a standard custom and practice is developed, this will be an important issue to monitor as we define what constitutes fair use of copyrighted images used in cyberspace.[30]

III. SOFTWARE

A. Reverse Engineering

[Add the following text at the end of the section.]

In *SAS Institute, Inc. v. World Programming Ltd.*,[31] the European Union's highest court reaffirmed the legality of reverse engineering on an international scale. In May 2012, the Court of Justice of the European Communities ruled that software companies cannot rely on copyright law to prohibit other software firms from reverse engineering computer programs. This decision was significant because it aligned with U.S. case law in establishing that reverse engineering software components is permissible, even if intermediate copying occurs.

---

[27]Pinterest, Copyright & Trademark, http://pinterest.com/about/copyright/ (last visited July 1, 2012).

[28]Pinterest, Terms & Privacy.

[29]*Id.*

[30]An online article in *Social Media Today* discusses whether Pinterest and its investors, rather than the individual user, would be pursued in court for infringing activities. *See* http://socialmediatoday.com/node/457517.

[31]Case No. C-406/10, 2012 E.R.C. (May 2, 2012), *available at* http://curia.europa. eu/juris/document/document.jsf?text&docid=122362&pageIndex=0&doclang=EN&m ode=lst&dir&occ=first&part=1&cid=115060.

The case involved a copyright infringement action brought by the U.S.-based company, SAS Institute, Inc. ("SAS"), "for infringement of copyright in computer programs and manuals relating to its computer database systems."[32] SAS created a language unique to the "SAS System" of statistical analysis that "enables users to write and run their own application programs in order to adapt the SAS System to work with their data (Scripts). Such Scripts are written in a language which is peculiar to the SAS System ('the SAS Language')."[33] World Programming Limited ("WPL") developed an "alternative software capable of executing application programs written in the SAS Language" so that users of the SAS System could run the Scripts they developed for the SAS System on WLP's new system.[34] Through this action, SAS ultimately petitioned the High Court of Justice of England and Wales, Chancery Division, to extend copyright protection to software program functions. Because the EU had not squarely addressed this issue since 1991 in its Directive 91/250,[35] the English Court of Justice stayed the action and referred to the EU's Court of Justice questions regarding how courts should interpret EU Directives and international treaties as they relate to reverse engineering of computer programs.[36]

The Court of Justice ultimately made the following rulings:

1. Article 1(2) of Council Directive 91/250/EEC of 14 May 1991 on the legal protection of computer programs must be interpreted as meaning that neither the functionality of a computer program nor the programming language and the format of data files used in a computer program in order to exploit certain of its functions constitute a form of expression of that program and, as such, are not protected by copyright in computer programs for the purposes of that directive.[37]

2. Article 5(3) of Directive 91/250 must be interpreted as meaning that a person who has obtained a copy of a computer program under a licence is entitled, without the authorisation of the owner of the copyright, to observe, study or test the functioning of that program so as to determine the ideas and principles which underlie any element of the program, in the case where that person carries out acts covered by that licence and acts of loading and running necessary for the use of the computer program, and on condition that that person does not infringe the exclusive rights of the owner of the copyright in that program.[38]

---

[32] Id. at ¶2.
[33] Id. at ¶23.
[34] Id. at ¶24.
[35] Council Directive 91/250/EEC of 14 May 1991 on the legal protection of computer programs, 1991 O.J. (L 122). The SAS Institute decision also references Directive 2001/29/EC of the European Parliament and of the Council of 22 May 2001 on the harmonisation of certain aspects of copyright and related rights in the information society, 2001 O.J. (L 167) which developed the principles and rules set forth in Directive 91/250/EEC and placed them in the context of the information society. See ruling 3 of the Court of Justice, infra.
[36] SAS Inst., Inc. v. World Programming Ltd., C-406/10.¶28. The Court of Justice does not refer to the actions of WPL as "reverse engineering" specifically, but instead explains what that process technically involves. Id.
[37] See also SAS Institute, Inc., ¶46.
[38] See also id. ¶¶61–62.

3. Article 2(a) of Directive 2001/29/EC of the European Parliament and of the Council of 22 May 2001 on the harmonisation of certain aspects of copyright and related rights in the information society must be interpreted as meaning that the reproduction, in a computer program or a user manual for that program, of certain elements described in the user manual for another computer program protected by copyright is capable of constituting an infringement of the copyright in the latter manual if—this being a matter for the national court to ascertain—that reproduction constitutes the expression of the intellectual creation of the author of the user manual for the computer program protected by copyright.[39]

The consistency of this decision with decisions of U.S. courts creates a helpful consistency in what the software industry can view as a permissible and an impermissible activity when re-engineering functionality and data formats.

B. Abstract-Filtration-Comparison Test

[Add the following text at the end of the section.]

Most recently, the Northern District of California did not even address the abstract-filtration-comparison test in its decision concerning the copyrightability of certain replicated elements of the Java Application Programming Interface (API). In *Oracle America, Inc. v. Google, Inc.*,[40] Oracle claimed that Google "had replicated the structure, sequence and organization of the overall code for … 37 API packages."[41] Following a trial, which was bifurcated between the jury and the court, the Central District of California had the final say when it concluded that the elements replicated by Google from the Java System were not copyrightable in the first place.[42]

Basic principles of copyright law—in lieu of complicated applications of copyright law as applied to software or to the Internet—carried the decision. The court first explained that "[a]s long as the specific code written to implement a method is different, anyone is free under the Copyright Act to write his or her own method to carry out exactly the same function or specification of any and all methods used in the Java API" because copyright law does not confer ownership over functionality or specification.[43] Furthermore, in instances, as here, where the method of specification in the declaration must be *identical* under the API's rules for functionality, "when there is only one way to write something, the merger

---

[39] *Id.* (final ruling); *see also id.* ¶ 70.

[40] No. 10-03561, 2012 WL 1964523, 2012 U.S. Dist. LEXIS 75896, 103 USPQ2d 1023 (N.D. Cal. May 31, 2012).

[41] *Id.* at *1, 2012 U.S. Dist. LEXIS 75897, at *7, 103 USPQ2d at 1025.

[42] *Id.* at *2, 2012 U.S. Dist. LEXIS 75897, at *8–9, 103 USPQ2d at 1025. The jury found Google had infringed Oracle's copyright, but was deadlocked on the decision as to whether the use was fair or *de minimus*. *See id.*, 2012 U.S. Dist. LEXIS 75897, at *7–8, 103 USPQ2d at 1025.

[43] *Id.* at *24, 2012 U.S. Dist. LEXIS 75897, at *70, 103 USPQ2d at 1042.

doctrine bars anyone from claiming exclusive copyright ownership of that expression."[44] Therefore, Java could not claim copyright protection in the declarations contained in its APIs.[45] Only Oracle's implementations were copyrightable, and Google had created its own implementations.[46]

Finally, the court emphasized that it is an explicit rule that names, titles, and short phrases are not copyrightable.[47] Because of this principle, the court reaffirmed its summary judgment order that copyright protection did not extend to Java's overall name organization and functionality.[48] Although the court recognized that Google

> could have [rearranged] the various methods under different groupings among the various classes and packages (even if the same names had been used).... In this sense, there were many ways to group the methods yet still duplicate the same range of functionality. But the names are more than just names—they are symbols in a command structure wherein ... the commands call[] into action a pre-assigned function. The overall name tree, of course, has creative elements but it is also a precise command structure—a utilitarian and functional set of symbols, each to carry out a pre-assigned function. This command structure is a system or method of operation under Section 102(b) of the Copyright Act and, therefore, cannot be copyrighted. Duplication of the command structure is necessary for interoperability.[49]

As a result, the Northern District of California dismissed Oracle's claims against Google.[50] In conclusion, however, the court clarified:

> This order does not hold that Java API packages are free for all to use without license. It does not hold that the structure, sequence and organization of all computer programs may be stolen. Rather, it holds on the specific facts of this case, the particular elements replicated by Google were free for all to use under the Copyright Act.[51]

Although Oracle will likely appeal this decision, it highlights the important role that basic principles of copyright law continue to play in defining the rights of copyright owners, even with the complications added through technology.

[44] Id. at *25, 2012 U.S. Dist. LEXIS 75897, at *73, 103 USPQ2d at 1042.
[45] Id., 2012 U.S. Dist. LEXIS 75897, at *73, 103 USPQ2d at 1042.
[46] Id., 2012 U.S. Dist. LEXIS 75897, at *74, 103 USPQ2d at 1043.
[47] Id. at *9, *25, 2012 U.S. Dist. LEXIS 75897, at *30–31, *73–74, 103 USPQ2d at 1031, 1042.
[48] Id. at *2, *25, 2012 U.S. Dist. LEXIS 75897, at *9–10, *74, 103 USPQ2d at 1026, 1043.
[49] Id. at *2, 2012 U.S. Dist. LEXIS 75897, at *10, 103 USPQ2d at 1026.
[50] Id. at *28, 2012 U.S. Dist. LEXIS 75897, at *85, 103 USPQ2d at 1045.
[51] Id., 2012 U.S. Dist. LEXIS 75897, at *84–85, 103 USPQ2d at 1045.

IV. MUSIC

A. Duplication, Distribution, and Public Performance: Digital Downloads

1. *Napster, LimeWire, and Other File-sharing Programs*

[Revision note.]

[By Order the U.S. District Court for Southern District of New York stated that it would issue an amended version of its opinion in *Arista LLC v. Lime Group LLC*, 715 F. Supp. 2d 481, 508 (S.D.N.Y. 2010). That opinion has, therefore, been withdrawn and superseded by 784 F. Supp. 2d 398 (S.D.N.Y. 2011); however, the court's revised opinion is substantively identical to its first opinion. The revisions to the court's opinion relate only to the parties' counsel and to footnote references. Nonetheless, for the avoidance of confusion, main volume footnotes 128, 130, 131, 132, 136, 142, and 145 should be replaced as follows.]

[128]*Id.* at 919. *See also* Arista Records LLC v. Lime Group LLC, 784 F. Supp. 2d 398, 424 (S.D.N.Y. 2011) ("In *Grokster*, the Supreme Court confirmed that inducement of copyright infringement constitutes a distinct cause of action.").

[130]*Lime Group LLC*, 784 F. Supp. 2d at 424. *See also* Arista Records, Inc. v. Mp3Board, Inc., 2002 WL 1997918, at *4, 2002 U.S. Dist. LEXIS 16165, at *12–13 (S.D.N.Y. Aug. 29, 2002); London-Sire Records, Inc. v. Doe 1, 542 F. Supp. 2d 153, 175 (D. Mass 2008).

[131]*Grokster*, 545 U.S. at 922; *Lime Group*, 784 F. Supp. 2d at 423.

[132]*Grokster*, 545 U.S. at 922; *Lime Group*, 784 F. Supp. 2d at 423.

[136]*Id.* at 937. *See also Lime Group LLC*, 784 F. Supp. 2d at 425 (explaining that the plaintiff must establish that the defendant (1) "engaged in purposeful conduct that encouraged copyright infringement" and (2) intended and encouraged the infringing conduct by third-party users).

[142]*Grokster Remand*, 454 F. Supp. 2d at 938–39; *Lime Group LLC*, 784 F. Supp. 2d at 425–31. In considering intent, the Southern District of New York in Lime Group also held that evidence of conduct falling outside of the statute of limitations "is relevant, probative, and admissible" to prove the motives of acts occurring within the statute of limitations. *Lime Group LLC*, 784 F. Supp. 2d at 418. Other admissible evidence of knowledge of infringing behavior and intent to induce direct infringement includes "(1) screenshots of software programs and related websites, (2) statements about LimeWire quoted in newspaper articles, and (3) strategy memos and talking points provided by LW's public relations firm." *Id.* at 421.

[145]*See Lime Group LLC*, 784 F. Supp. 2d at 434–35.

4. *"The Cloud"*

[Replace the final paragraph of the section on page 280 with the following text.]

Although *MP3Tunes* began to clarify the specific applications of copyright law to the storage of music in via cloud, many questions remain. There has been no opportunity for appellate review of the case[52] and such opportunity may not present itself. On June 25, 2012, the Southern District of New York stayed the copyright infringement in light of MP3 Tunes' Chapter 7 Bankruptcy petition.[53] But outside of the specific facts of this particular case, who owns the data being stored in the cloud? Who owns the software and interface used to access, download, or display a purportedly infringing work? Which party infringed the copyrights? For jurisdictional purposes, where is "the cloud" located? And do any statutory defenses shield the owners of this software from liability?

Publishing and digital music service providers are not sitting idly by awaiting court action and are, instead, making strides to authorize the reproduction and distribution of musical compositions through cloud services as well as through other digital methods. In the Copyright Royalty Board's ("CRB's") Section 115 rate-setting proceedings for the compulsory use of musical works in physical and digital phonorecords,[54] these companies voluntarily chose to reach an agreement on statutory rates for certain new categories of services developed since the last proceedings five years earlier or services that are likely to launch over the course of the next five years.[55] In the April 10, 2012 settlement proposal submitted to the Copyright Royalty Judges and published in the *Federal Register* for notice and comment on May 17, 2012, publishing and digital companies proposed to establish "rates and terms of royalty payments for certain reproductions or distributions of musical works through limited offerings, mixed service bundles, music bundles, paid locker services, and

---

[52]Capital Records, Inc. v. MP3Tunes, LLC, Memorandum and Order, No. 07 Civ. 9931, 2012 U.S. Dist. LEXIS 8984 (S.D.N.Y. Jan. 9, 2012) (denying EMI's request to certify the issues for interlocutory review, finding that although its "October 25, 2011 Memorandum & Order may involve a 'substantial ground for difference of opinion,' particularly in light of the Copyright Office's recent determination that the DMCA safe harbors do not apply to pre-1972 recordings," this was not a controlling issue of law in the case).

[53]Capital Records, Inc. v. MP3Tunes, LLC, Memorandum and Order, No. 07 Civ. 9931, 2012 U.S. Dist. LEXIS 87718 (S.D.N.Y. June 25, 2012).

[54]With the passage of the Digital Performance Right in Sound Recordings Act of 1995, Pub. L. No. 104-39, 109 Stat. 336, Congress amended 17 U.S.C. §115 to clarify that the Section 115 mechanical license for musical compositions extended to digital phonorecord deliveries. *See* 17 U.S.C. §115(c)(3). In January 2011, the Copyright Royalty Judges ("CRJs") published notice to commence proceedings to set the new compulsory mechanical license rates for January 1, 2013 through December 31, 2017, and requested parties timely indicate participation in the process. 76 Fed. Reg. 590 (Jan. 5, 2011), *available at* http://www.loc.gov/crb/fedreg/2011/76fr590.pdf; *see* 77 Fed. Reg. 29,259 (May 17, 2012) (to be codified at 37 C.F.R. pt. 385), *available at* http://www.loc.gov/crb/fedreg/2012/77fr29259.pdf; *see also* 17 U.S.C. §803(b)(3) (requiring the three-month review process).

[55]77 Fed. Reg. 29,259–70 (May 17, 2012); *In re Adjustment or Determination of Compulsory License Rates for Making and Distributing Phonorecords*, Dkt. No. 2011-3 CRB Phonorecords II, Motion to Adopt Settlement (April 10, 2012), *available at* http://us.practicallaw.com/cs/Satellite?blobcol=urldata&blobheader=application%2Fpdf&blobkey=id&blobtable=MungoBlobs&blobwhere=1247570745597&ssbinary=true.

purchased content locker services."[56] "The Cloud" is most likely implicated in a locker service, which is defined as "a service providing access to sound recordings of musical works in the form of interactive streams, permanent digital downloads, restricted downloads or ringtones, where the service has reasonably determined that phonorecords of the applicable sound recordings have been purchased by the end user or are otherwise in the possession of the end user prior to the end user's first request to access such sound recordings by means of the service."[57] Although the CRB has not yet adopted this settlement proposal and we have not had the opportunity to observe the practical implications of this additional compulsory licensing structure on these new services, the fact that publishing companies and digital music service providers have agreed to a statutory mechanical rate for musical compositions reproduced or distributed through locker services and other digital platforms makes it clear that a license is indeed required—even when reproduction or distribution occurs through use of a cloud—and that the largest and most powerful companies affected are prepared to stand behind this requirement.

Digital music service providers' willingness to acknowledge the need to license music used through these services and to accept the creation of a compulsory licensing structure is likely tied to the publishing companies' willingness to agree to a rate structure compatible with realistic payments that digital service providers can afford at this time. First, the rate is a percentage of revenue the service provider collects from users and from sponsorships and commissions, including advertising revenue directly related to such services.[58] This revenue basis is in lieu of a per-reproduction penny rate. Second, the proposed structure allows service providers to subtract the applicable performance royalties paid, including payments pursuant to 17 U.S.C. §114, as explained in Section IV.B.4 below,[59] which again recognizes the practical hurdles digital music service providers face in complying with copyright licensing requirements.[60] Third, the royalty rate is specifically tailored to the type of service through which the authorized activities occur, recognizing that a cookie-cutter licensing structure may be impractical for the seemingly limitless technologies that may develop towards the use of music on the Internet.[61] The submitted proposal perhaps reflects a growing recognition of both publishing companies and digital music service providers that each increasingly relies on the other for its viability and that a joint resolution is less expensive and more comprehensive than decisions made by a court or by an appointed government body. We must now wait to see whether the CRB will adopt this significant settlement.

---

[56] 77 Fed. Reg. 29,263 (May 17, 2012).

[57] Id. at 29,264.

[58] Id. at 29,265–66.

[59] See Section IV.B.4 in the main volume.

[60] 77 Fed. Reg. 29,265–66.

[61] Id.

B. Digital Performance of Music: Audio Streaming

[Revise the Section IV.B.iv heading to read as follows.]

4. *Section 114 Licensing Structure for Non-Interactive Services [Revised Heading]*

[Revise the Section IV.C heading to read as follows.]

C. First Sale Doctrine and Digital Distributors [Revised Heading]

[Redesignate Section V.C to Section VI as follows.]

VI. VIDEO [REDESIGNATED]

[Redesignate Section V.D to Section VI.A as follows.]

A. Copying of Motion Pictures: Protection Against Circumvention of Safeguards to Prevent Copying of Audiovisual Content [Redesignated]

[Redesignate Section V.E to Section VI.B as follows.]

B. Video Content Service Providers [Redesignated]

[Add the following text after the full paragraph on page 298.]

The Second Circuit accepted on appeal *Viacom International, Inc. v. YouTube, Inc.*,[62] along with its companion case, *Football Association Premier League, Ltd. v. YouTube*,[63] "to clarify the contours of the 'safe harbor' pro-

---

[62] 676 F.3d 19, 102 USPQ2d 1283 (2d Cir. 2012).

[63] In *Football Association Premier League, Ltd. v. YouTube*, brought in the Southern District of New York, music publisher plaintiffs alleged that YouTube infringed the publisher's copyrights through the unauthorized use of copyrighted musical works on the Web site.

Following the plaintiffs' appeal of the district court's decision to the Second Circuit Court of Appeals, the National Music Publishers' Association and certain publishers entered into a settlement agreement with YouTube. In exchange for dismissal of all claims, YouTube entered into a three year licensing agreement with NMPA and agreed to pay a $4,000,000 recoupable advance pool to music publishers opting into the settlement and licensing agreement by January 16, 2012 (with the advance to be prorated among music publishers based on their respective share of licensing income). Publishers will also be paid a royalty of 15% net advertising revenue for videos uploaded by users that incorporate the licensed rights and embody at least one sound recording, and 50% of

vision of the Digital Millennium Copyright Act (DMCA) that limits the liability of online service providers for copyright infringement that occurs 'by reason of the storage at the direction of a user of material that resides on a system or network controlled or operated by or for the service provider.'"[64] The court held as follows:

[1] [T]he District Court correctly held that the §512(c) safe harbor requires knowledge or awareness of specific infringing activity, but we vacate the order granting summary judgment because a reasonable jury could find that YouTube had actual knowledge or awareness of specific infringing activity on its website....

[2] [T]he District Court erred by interpreting the "right and ability to control" provision to require "item-specific" knowledge.

[3] Finally, we affirm the District Court's holding that three of the challenged YouTube software functions fall within the safe harbor for infringement that occurs "by reason of" user storage; we remand for further fact-finding with respect to a fourth software function.[65]

In reaching the above conclusion, the Second Circuit first affirmed that a service provider must meet all threshold criteria for safe harbor protection,[66] as well as the requirements for the particular safe harbor at issue, in this case that in Section 512(c).[67] With this background, the court

---

net advertising revenues (less certain deductible expenses) for user-generated content that incorporates a cover recording. The Harry Fox Agency will administer this licensing arrangement for a fee of 7.5%. *See* www.youtubelicenseoffer.com (last visited July 2, 2012). YouTube also implemented its own licensing arrangement for individual music publishers.

[64] *Viacom Int'l*, 676 F.3d at 25, 102 USPQ2d at 1285 (quoting 17 U.S.C. §512(c)). The court noted that "[t]hese related cases present a series of significant questions of statutory construction." *Id.* at 26, 102 USPQ2d at 1285.

[65] *Id.*, 102 USPQ2d at 1285.

[66] *Id.* at 27, 102 USPQ2d at 1286; *see also* 17 U.S.C. §512(k)(1)(B) (definition of "service provider"); *id.* §512(i)(1)(A) (conditions of eligibility); *id.* §512(i)(1)(B), (i)(2) (satisfaction of technical measures used by copyright owners to identify to identify or protect copyrighted works).

[67] Under 17 U.S.C. §512(c)(1), the safe harbor protection applies to the service provider who:

(A)(i) does not have actual knowledge that the material or an activity using the material on the system or network is infringing;

(ii) in the absence of such actual knowledge, is not aware of facts or circumstances from which infringing activity is apparent; or

(iii) upon obtaining such knowledge or awareness, acts expeditiously to remove, or disable access to, the material;

(B) does not receive a financial benefit directly attributable to the infringing activity, in a case in which the service provider has the right and ability to control such activity; and

(C) upon notification of claimed infringement as described in paragraph (3), responds expeditiously to remove, or disable access to, the material that is claimed to be infringing or to be the subject of infringing activity.

The Second Circuit also affirmed, quite significantly, that "a finding of safe harbor application necessarily protects a defendant from all affirmative claims for monetary

then addressed the most important issue on appeal: whether the Section 512(c) safe harbor "requires 'actual knowledge' or 'aware[ness]' of facts or circumstances indicating 'specific and identifiable infringements.'"[68] The Second Circuit looked directly at the structure of the statute and its removal obligation, which expressly "contemplates knowledge or awareness of specific infringing material" in order to remove such items. In accordance with the district court, the Second Circuit interpreted the statutory language and structure of these provisions to mean that a service provider's general knowledge of possible infringements does not disqualify it from safe harbor protection.[69]

This was the same conclusion reached in December 2011 by the Ninth Circuit in *UMG Recordings, Inc. v. Shelter Capital Partners, LLC.*[70] And like the Ninth Circuit, the Second Circuit in *Viacom International, Inc.* also addressed the meaning of the "red flag provision" of Section 512(c), which provides protection only if the service provider, "in the absence of such actual knowledge, is not aware of facts or circumstances from which infringing activity is apparent."[71] According to the court, this "red-flag" provision does not disqualify the service provider from safe harbor protection just because the service provider has a more general knowledge that infringing activity could potentially occur through the service.[72] The Second Circuit provided a new perspective on this conclusion, however. "The difference between actual and red flag knowledge is ... not between specific and generalized knowledge, but instead between a subjective and an objective standard."[73] Actual knowledge is a question of whether the service provider was subjectively aware of specific infringements.[74] Red flag knowledge is whether the reasonable objective facts or circumstances would lead a reasonable person to have actual knowledge of specific infringements.[75] As such, the Second Circuit agreed with the district court's interpretation of the knowledge requirement for applying Section 512(c) and found the burden rests with the copyright holder.

Conversely, the Second Circuit disagreed with the district court's entire dismissal of the plaintiffs' claims that YouTube had actual knowledge of specific infringing works. Even under the Second Circuit's interpretation of the safe harbor, there was sufficient evidence to raise "a

---

relief," including claims for direct, vicarious, and contributory liability. *Viacom Int'l, Inc.,* 676 F.3d at 41, 102 USPQ2d at 1296.

[68] *Id.* at 30, 102 USPQ2d at 1288 (quoting the district court decision, Viacom Int'l, Inc. v. YouTube, Inc., 718 F. Supp. 2d 514, 523, 95 USPQ2d 1766, 1773 (S.D.N.Y., 2010)).

[69] *Id.* at 30–31 102 USPQ2d at 1288.

[70] 667 F.3d 1022, 1037–38, 101 USPQ2d 1001, 1011 ("Requiring specific knowledge of particular infringing activity makes good sense in the context of the DMCA ....").

[71] 17 U.S.C. §512(c)(1)(A)(ii).

[72] *Viacom Int'l, Inc.,* 676 F.3d at 31, 102 USPQ2d at 1288–89; *see UMG Recordings, Inc.,* 667 F.3d at 1038, 101 USPQ2d at 1012 (finding the burden remains with the copyright holder and that general knowledge of hosting copyrightable material is insufficient to constitute a red flag).

[73] *Viacom Int'l, Inc.,* 676 F.3d at 31, 102 USPQ2d at 1289.

[74] *Id.,* 102 USPQ2d at 1289.

[75] *Id.,* 102 USPQ2d at 1289.

material issue of fact regarding YouTube's knowledge or awareness of specific instances of infringement."[76] Sufficient evidence to overcome summary judgment in this instance was a few select internal emails from YouTube executives with occasional references to clips containing material owned by the plaintiffs and containing questions regarding whether to proceed with takedown.[77] Nonetheless, the court narrowed this decision by specifying that it was unclear whether the referenced clips in the emails were even about the particular video clips at issue in the present case and whether the emails suggested actual knowledge of specific infringement.[78] The court remanded these issue for a determination by the district court.[79] The Second Circuit's decision on this matter is significant in that it sticks strictly to the specificity requirement for knowledge. Emails specifically referencing a plaintiff's material in general is insufficient. An email may be relevant only if it references the specific intellectual property and clips at issue in the case.

The court also addressed for the first time two additional issues. First, noting that the statute does not speak to this doctrine of willful blindness, the court reviewed the application of the common law doctrine in the DMCA context. The court held that the doctrine of willful blindness "may be applied, in appropriate circumstances, to demonstrate knowledge or awareness of specific instances of infringement under the DMCA."[80] However, the court noted that the doctrine is limited by Section 512(m), which provides that the safe harbor is not contingent upon affirmatively monitoring the services provided.[81]

The court then considered the meaning of the "right and ability to control" the infringing activity under Section 512(c)(1)(B). YouTube argued for the Second Circuit to adopt the same interpretation as the Ninth Circuit[82]—that "until [the service provider] becomes aware of specific unauthorized material, it cannot exercise its 'power or authority' over the specific infringing item. In practical terms, it does not have the kind of ability to control infringing activity the statute contemplates."[83] The Second Circuit disagreed with YouTube and the Ninth Circuit, however, explaining that the foregoing construction "import[s] a specific knowledge requirement" and renders it "duplicative of §512(c)(1)(A)."[84] The court also rejected the proposed interpretation of the plaintiffs, who argued that the "right and ability to control" was a codification of vicarious

---

[76] Id. at 34, 102 USPQ2d at 1291.

[77] Id. at 33–34, 102 USPQ2d at 1290–91.

[78] Id. at 34, 102 USPQ2d at 1291.

[79] Id., 102 USPQ2d at 1291.

[80] Id. at 35, 102 USPQ2d at 1292.

[81] Id., 102 USPQ2d at 1292.

[82] Id. at 36, 102 USPQ2d at 1292–93; see UMG Recordings, Inc., 667 F.3d at 1043, 101 USPQ2d at 1016 ("[W]e hold that the 'right and ability to control' under §512(c) requires control over specific infringing activity the provider knows about. A service provider's general right and ability to remove materials from its services is, alone, insufficient.").

[83] Id. at 1041, 101 USPQ2d at 1015.

[84] Viacom Int'l, Inc., 676 F.3d at 36, 102 USPQ2d at 1293.

liability.[85] According to the court, such an interpretation would render
Section 512(c) internally inconsistent, as the statute "actually presumes
that service providers have the ability to 'block … access' to infringing
material."[86] Unfortunately, the court provides little guidance on the appropriate interpretation of this provision. It cites only to the examples
provided in *Perfect 10, Inc. v. Cybernet Ventures, Inc.*,[87] where there the Web
site had a monitoring program to instruct users on the appearance and
content of the Web site, and *Metro-Goldwyn-Mayer Studios, Inc. v. Grokster,
Ltd.*,[88] where the purposeful, culpable expression of conduct was the basis
for imposing liability.[89] These two examples involved "a service provider
exerting substantial influence on the activities of users, without necessarily—or even frequently—acquiring knowledge of specific infringing
activity," and the court provided this as its only guidance in remanding
the case to the district court for a determination of whether this provision
applies.[90]

Finally, the Second Circuit aligns with other courts, including the
Ninth Circuit's most recent opinion on the matter, in its interpretation
of the meaning of "infringement of copyright by reason of storage at the
direction of a user" sufficient to invoke the Section 512(c) safe harbor.[91]
In *UMG Recordings, Inc.*, the Ninth Circuit rejected the plaintiffs' argument that "by reason of storage" should mean that "infringement must
be proximately caused by the storage,"[92] and explained that such a read-
ing would create an internal inconsistency in Section 512(c).[93] Section
512(c) is not confined to Web hosts and has a detailed notice and take-
down procedure and references disabling access to infringing materials,
"presuppos[ing] that service providers will provide access to users' stored
material."[94] Therefore, where the service provider does not "actively participate in or supervise file uploading," the Ninth Circuit found that liability from transcoding and playback arise "by reason of the storage at
the direction of a user."[95]

The Second Circuit looked to the Ninth Circuit's reasoning in like-
wise finding the safe harbor is not lost when a service provider can trans-
code videos into a standard display format, playback the video on "watch"
pages, or see "related" videos featured on the page.[96] The court explained

---

[85] *Id.* at 36, 102 USPQ2d at 1293.
[86] *Id.* at 37, 102 USPQ2d at 1293.
[87] 213 F. Supp. 2d 1146 (C.D. Cal. 2002).
[88] 545 U.S. 913, 75 USPQ2d 1001 (2005).
[89] *Viacom Int'l, Inc.*, 676 F.3d at 38, 102 USPQ2d at 1294.
[90] *Id.*, 102 USPQ2d at 1294.
[91] *See* 17 U.S.C. §512(c)(1) .
[92] *UMG Recordings, Inc.*, 667 F.3d at 1032, 101 USPQ2d at 1007.
[93] *Id.* at 1033, 101 USPQ2d at 1008.
[94] *Id.*, 101 USPQ2d at 1008.
[95] *Id.* at 1035, 101 USPQ2d at 1010.
[96] *Viacom Int'l, Inc.*, 676 F.3d at 39, 102 USPQ2d at 1294. The court also refused
to issue an advisory opinion on syndication to compatible mobile devices and instead
remanded the issue to the district court for a determination of whether any of the
applicable videos were actually syndicated for such use. *Id.* at 40, 102 USPQ2d at 1295.

that "§512(c) 'is clearly meant to cover more than mere electronic storage lockers,'"[97] and the challenged functions of transcoding and playback are merely responses to requests by users. With respect to the "related videos" functions, the court found the safe harbor protection remains in place because the video algorithm creating these features requires no input from YouTube employees.[98] The Second Circuit, therefore, upheld the district court's grant of summary judgment on these issues in favor of YouTube.

---

[97] *Id.* at 39, 102 USPQ2d at 1295 (quoting UMG Recordings, Inc. v. Veoh Networks, Inc., 620 F. Supp. 2d 1081, 1088, 89 USPQ2d 1449, 1455 (C.D. Cal. 2008)).

[98] *Id.* at 39–40, 102 USPQ2d at 1295.

PART III

PROTECTING THE KEY ELEMENTS OF A WEB SITE

7

Unique Online Trademark Issues*

Howard S. Hogan
Gibson, Dunn & Crutcher LLP
Washington, D.C.

Stephen W. Feingold
Kilpatrick Townsend & Stockton LLP
New York, New York

*The authors gratefully acknowledge the invaluable assistance of Ashley S. Boizelle, an associate with the Washington, D.C. office of Gibson Dunn, in the research and writing of this chapter update.

II. Confusion Online

[58][Add the following text at the end of footnote 58.] *See also* AR Pillow Inc. v. Cottrell, No. C11-1962, 2012 U.S. Dist. LEXIS 33488, at *5 (W.D. Wash. Mar. 13, 2012) (citing Google Webmaster Central Blog for the fact that Google no longer relies on metatags to determine search results.)

A. Types of Confusion on the Internet

3. *Initial Interest Confusion*

c. *Cases Rejecting the Doctrine of Initial Interest Confusion*

[112][Add the following text at the end of footnote 112.] ; 3 Form, Inc. v. Lumicor, Inc., No. 2:09-CV-990, 2012 U.S. Dist. LEXIS 27504, at *26 (D. Utah Mar. 1, 2012) ("[T]he fact that a competitor's search results appear as one of many options when conducting a web search will not confuse consumers, as they will have different appearances.").

[113][Add the following text at the end of footnote 113.] *But see* Scooter Store, Inc. v. Spinlife.com, LLC, No. 2:10-cv-18, 2011 U.S. Dist. LEXIS 148580, at *10 (S.D. Ohio Dec. 21, 2011) (declining to rely on *1-800 Contacts, Inc. v. Lens.com, Inc.* for the proposition that purchases from Google AdWords are never actionable as trademark infringement).

[117][In footnote 117, replace the *Sensient Technologies* citation with the following.] 613 F.3d 754, 96 USPQ2d 1164 (8th Cir. 2010), *cert. denied*, 131 S. Ct. 1603, 179 L. Ed. 2d 500, 2011 U.S. LEXIS 2081 (2011).

[121][Add the following text at the end of footnote 121.] ; Rosetta Stone Ltd. v. Google, Inc., 676 F.3d 144, 159–60, 102 USPQ2d 1473, 1484–85 (4th Cir. 2012) (finding consumer sophistication factor did not favor Google as a matter of law despite the high price paid for the Rosetta Stone product and time commitment required to learn a foreign language; testimony that customers purchased counterfeit Rosetta Stone software from Google's sponsored links and an internal Google study "reflecting that even well-educated, seasoned Internet consumers are confused by the nature of Google's sponsored links and are sometimes even unaware that sponsored links are, in actuality, advertisements" created a disputed issue of fact as to consumer sophistication on summary judgment.)

[Add the following text at the end of the section.]

In *Ascentive, LLC v. Opinion Corp.*,[1] the U.S. District Court for the Eastern District of New York denied a motion for preliminary injunction,

---

[1]No. 10 Civ. 4433, 2011 WL 6181452, 2011 U.S. Dist. LEXIS 143081 (E.D.N.Y. Dec. 13, 2011). This case is also discussed in Section VI.B.2 of this supplement, *infra*.

finding it "unlikely" that the defendant's gripe Web site ("PissedConsumer") would cause initial interest confusion with that of the plaintiffs and suggested that the plaintiffs seek recourse from the search engines themselves—not the court—for search results manipulated by the defendant. The plaintiffs complained that the defendant used their marks in its addresses (e.g., "Ascentive.PissedConsumer.Com" and "Dormia.PissedConsumer.com") as well as in metadata and Web site content.[2] Distinguishing *Brookfield*, the court held that the defendant "cannot divert Internet users away from plaintiffs' sites because PissedConsumer's site is not in competition with those of plaintiffs," and the defendant's Web pages were critical of the plaintiffs' products and thus did not suggest any affiliation or sponsorship by the plaintiffs.[3]

The court also rejected the plaintiffs' argument that the defendant's reposting of consumer complaints on Twitter to increase its Web site visibility on Internet search lists violated the Lanham Act. The court explained:

> While it may be—and likely is—the case that PissedConsumer's SEO practices are intended to make its webpages seem more relevant to search engines than they actually are and these methods may indeed violate the search engines' terms of service, the remedy for this conduct is not trademark law but instead with the search engines themselves....
>
> If the search engines conclude that PissedConsumer's SEO practices are indeed in violation of their terms of service or guidelines, they can take certain steps to punish PissedConsumer including lowering the site's place in their search result lists or removing the site from their lists completely—the so called "death penalty."[4]

The court also noted that current search engines generally do not use metatags to determine search results as they did at the time of the *Brookfield* decision.[5] Regardless, the court concluded that placement on the search engine list was "ultimately irrelevant" since consumers who visit the defendant's Web site would not likely believe that the site was affiliated with the plaintiffs anyway.[6]

III. TRADEMARK OWNERS' DUTY TO ENFORCE ON THE INTERNET

A. The Duty to Police Generally

[Add the following text at the end of the last paragraph of the section on page 338.]

---

[2]*Ascentive, LLC*, 2011 WL 6181452, 2011 U.S. Dist. LEXIS 143081, at *2–3.
[3]2011 U.S. Dist. LEXIS 143081, at *36–39.
[4]2011 U.S. Dist. LEXIS 143081, at *47–48.
[5]2011 U.S. Dist. LEXIS 143081, at *44–45.
[6]2011 U.S. Dist. LEXIS 143081, at *49.

For example, in *Anthony's Pizza & Pasta International, Inc. v. Anthony's Pizza Holding Co.*,[7] the Court of Appeals for the Federal Circuit affirmed a finding of the Trademark Trial and Appeal Board that Anthony's Pizza Holding Co.'s (APHC's) ANTHONY'S COAL-FIRED PIZZA was confusingly similar to Anthony's Pizza & Pasta International's (APPI's) existing registration for ANTHONY'S PIZZA & PASTA, despite the presence of a similar ANTHONY'S PIZZA THE WORLD'S GREATEST design mark on the federal register. Importantly, the court reviewed evidence that the senior user "may not have adequately policed its mark," and concluded that there was no "evidence of a mark confusingly similar" because the senior user "sought to minimize potential confusion with a previously registered third-party mark through its participation in a co-existence agreement that sought to establish distinct channels of trade."[8] The Federal Circuit noted that "[t]his court has specifically endorsed coexistence agreements that accept the parties' reasonable appraisal of marketplace conditions."[9]

The court also found that the senior user, APPI, could prevent registration of APHC's ANTHONY'S COAL-FIRED PIZZA mark even though the junior user was the party named "Anthony" in this litigation. "[A] junior user's right to use his name 'must give way to the more compelling public and private interests involved in avoiding likelihood of confusion.'"[10]

IV. Domain Names as Trademarks Generally

[187][Add the following text before the *Area 55* citation in the first paragraph of footnote 187.]; Levi Strauss & Co. v. Papikian Enters., Inc., No. C 10-05051, 2011 WL 5192237, at *2–4, 2011 U.S. Dist. LEXIS 126223, at *14 (N.D. Cal. Nov. 1, 2011) (unpublished) (triable issue as to whether domains 501USA.com and 501USA.net, used for a Web site that sold discontinued or out-of-stock Levi Strauss brand jeans, infringed Levi Strauss trademarks);

B.   Domain Case Names

1.   *Generic and Descriptive Domain Names*

[243a][Add the following new footnote 243a at the end of the last paragraph of Section IV.B.1 on page 348.] *See, e.g., In re* Hotels.com, L.P., 573 F.3d 1300, 1304–06, 91 USPQ2d 1532, 1536–37 (Fed. Cir. 2009) (TTAB properly refused registration of "hotels.com" as generic, despite 64 decla-

---

[7] 2009 TTAB LEXIS 718, 95 USPQ2d 1271 (T.T.A.B. Nov. 10, 2009), *aff'd per curiam,* Appeal No. 2010-1191, 415 F. App'x 222, 2010 U.S. App. LEXIS 23898 (Fed Cir. Nov 18, 2010).
[8] *Id.,* 415 F. App'x at 225, 2010 U.S. App. LEXIS 23898, at *7–8.
[9] *Id.,* 2010 U.S. App. LEXIS 23898, at *9.
[10] *Id.,* 2010 U.S. App. LEXIS 23898, at *8 (quoting Ford Motor Co. v. Ford, 462 F.2d 1405, 1407, 174 USPQ 456, 458 (C.C.P.A. 1972)). The court noted that the instant marks did not involve either a full name or a last name.

rations and survey evidence showing that the relevant public viewed the mark as distinctive, where the evidence also showed a "large number of similar usages of 'hotels' with a dot-com suffix, as well as the common meaning and dictionary definition of 'hotels' and the standard usage of '.com' to show a commercial internet domain").

V. USE OF TRADEMARKS ON THE INTERNET TO SUPPORT REGISTRATION

B. Trademarks for Goods

2. Dell's Application

[Revise the Section V.B.2.c heading to read as follows.]

    c. TTAB Decisions Discussing Prominence of a Mark on a Web Site [Revised Heading]

VI. DOMAIN NAMES IN TRADEMARK INFRINGEMENT

B. Likelihood of Confusion

1. *Cases Generally Finding Likelihood of Confusion*

[409][Add the following text at the end of footnote 409.] ; *cf.* Carnivale v. Staub Design LLC, No. 11-1124, 456 F. App'x 104, 106–07, 2012 U.S. App. LEXIS 137, at *3–5 (3d Cir. Jan. 4, 2012) (where the defendants' domain www.theaffordablehouse.com was confusingly similar to the plaintiff's domain www.affordablehouse.com, district court erred in drawing an inference of the defendants' bad faith based on nothing more than an unsupported hypothesis that the defendants "'may have' or 'might have been motivated' to divert customers away from [the plaintiff's] website").

2. *Cases Generally Not Finding Likelihood of Confusion*

[Add the following text at the end of the section.]

Some courts have reached the same result for the use of a plaintiff's mark as a component of a URL's domain or subdomain, where other portions of the URL dispel any likelihood of consumer confusion. For example, in *Ascentive, LLC v. Opinion Corp.,*[11] the owners of the Internet

---

[11]No. 10 Civ. 4433, 2011 WL 6181452, 2011 U.S. Dist. LEXIS 143081 (E.D.N.Y. Dec. 13, 2011). This case is also discussed in Section II.A.3.c. of this supplement, *supra.*

domains www.ascentive.com and www.dormia.com brought Lanham Act claims against the owner of PissedConsumer, a consumer gripe site that featured critical consumer commentary at its subdomains (such as Ascentive.PissedConsumer.com and Dormia.PissedConsumer.com). In denying the plaintiffs' request for a preliminary injunction, the district court concluded that there was no likelihood of consumer confusion where the domain name "makes clear that it is not affiliated with trademarks the domain name incorporates and indeed is critical of the companies that own the marks."[12]

VII. OVERVIEW OF DIFFERENT TYPES OF DOMAIN NAME TRADEMARK DISPUTES

[Replace the first paragraph of the section on page 373 with the following text.]

Domain name disputes involving trademark law issues assume a variety of forms, though the practices that lead to these disputes are generally variations on a theme. To better understand potential legal responses available to trademark owners, it is useful to understand the different kinds of abuses that prompt trademark litigation in the online context.

[Add the following text at the end of the first sentence of the *Cybersquatting* paragraph on page 373.]

and then attempting to profit from ownership of the domain name by either ransoming the domain name back to the trademark holder or by using the domain name to divert business from the trademark holder to the domain name holder.[13] Conduct of this sort has been described as the "Internet version of a land grab."[14]

[426][Add the following text at the beginning of footnote 426.] Indeed, in passing ACPA, Congress was aware of individuals attaching obscene or pornographic material to an infringing domain name in order to tarnish the mark. *See* S. REP. No. 106-140, at 6 (1999), *available at* http://www.gpo.gov/fdsys/pkg/CRPT-106srpt140/pdf/CRPT-106srpt140.pdf. *See also*

---

[12]*Ascentive, LLC*, 2011 WL 6181452, at *8, 2011 U.S. Dist. LEXIS 143081, at *29. *See also* Toyota Motor Sales, U.S.A., Inc. v. Tabari, 610 F.3d 1171, 1176, 95 USPQ2d 1702, 1705–06 (9th Cir. 2010) (injunction that prohibited the defendants from using "domain names that on their face dispel any confusion as to sponsorship or endorsement" was "plainly overbroad").

[13]*See* DaimlerChrysler v. The Net, Inc., 388 F.3d 201, 204, 72 USPQ2d 1912, 1914 (6th Cir. 2004).

[14]Interstellar Starship Servs., Ltd. v. Epix, Inc., 304 F.3d 936, 946, 64 USPQ2d 1514, 1521 (9th Cir. 2002).

[429a][Add the following new footnote 429a at the end of the first sentence of the *Typosquatting* paragraph on page 374.] *See* Shields v. Zuccarini, 254 F.3d 476, 483, 59 USPQ2d 1207, 1211–12 (3d Cir. 2001); *see also* Green v. Fornario, 486 F.3d 100, 103 n.5, 82 USPQ2d 1681, 1684 n.5 (3d Cir. 2007) (describing typosquatting as a "subgenre of cybersquatting" that "involves registering a domain name that is but a letter or two off from a distinctive mark") (citing *Shields v. Zuccarini*); Andy Johnson-Laird, *Looking Forward, Legislating Backward?*, 4 J. SMALL & EMERGING BUS. L. 95, 101 (2000) (explaining that typosquatting, a twist on cybersquatting, is the registering of "mistyped variants of popular domain names to catch the electronic crumbs dropped by careless web surfers") (citing example).

[435][Add the following text at the end of footnote 435.] ; *see also* Webadvisor v. Bank of Am. Corp., No. 10-2163, 448 F. App'x 95, 98, 2011 U.S. App. LEXIS 21648, at *6–7 (2d Cir. Oct. 26, 2011) (holding that individual who admittedly sought to "acquire high value domain names and park them with domain parking service providers to generate pay-per-click revenue" violated ACPA because "[h]is business model relied upon diverting internet users ... to his own website—which contained content that could tarnish the infringed marks, or at the very least was not what the searchers sought to find—in order to profit from the 'pay-per-click revenue' that their increased web traffic would bring his site").

VIII. TRADEMARK DILUTION ONLINE

B. Blurring

[Replace the second and third sentence of the second full paragraph and footnote 474 on page 379 with the following text and footnote.]

At least one court has held that a trial court cannot enter judgment against a dilution claim solely based on evidence that the junior user's action served to increase the public's identification of the famous mark with its core product or service.[15] Instead, courts have determined that although not every factor will be relevant in every case, and not every blurring claim will require extensive discussion of each factor, a trial court is required to offer "a sufficient indication of which factors it has found persuasive and explain why they are persuasive."[16]

---

[15] *See* Rosetta Stone Ltd. v. Google, Inc., 676 F.3d 144, 170–71, 102 USPQ2d 1473, 1493 (4th Cir. 2012) (noting that even where evidence indicates that public recognition of the defendants' product increased, a court must consider other dilution factors and must focus its inquiry not on actual injury but on the "*likelihood* of dilution") (emphasis in original). *Rosetta Stone* is also discussed in Sections IX.C.2, X.I.2, and XVI.B.5 in this chapter of the supplement.

[16] *Rosetta Stone*, 676 F.3d at 170, 102 USPQ2d at 1492–93 (quoting *Louis Vuitton*, 507 F.3d at 266, 84 USPQ2d at 1978).

IX. TRADEMARKS IN SEARCH ENGINES AND INTERNET ADVERTISING

A. Use of Trademarks as Metatags

2. *Permissible Use*

[Add the following text at the end of the section.]

A recent decision from the U.S. District Court for the District of Utah illustrates this point. In *3 Form, Inc. v. Lumicor, Inc.,*[17] the court granted summary judgment in dismissing trademark infringement claims based on a company's use of a competitor's name in metatags. In particular, the court held that because the trademark appeared only in the invisible metatags and not in any visible form on the defendant's Web site, "the only effect that a metatag could have on search results is that it *might* make [the defendant's] website appear among the results listed.... [T]he fact that a competitor's search results appear as one of many options when conducting a web search will not confuse customers, as they will have different appearances."[18] As technology advances, however, it is always possible that metatags will be used in new and more confusing ways.

[Revise the Section IX.B heading to read as follows.]

B. Pop-Up Advertisements as Trademark Use [Revised Heading]

C. Search Engine Advertising and Trademarks

2. *Likelihood of Confusion*

[529][Add the following text at the beginning of footnote 529 after *See, e.g.,*] Rosetta Stone v. Google, Inc., 676 F.3d 144, 102 USPQ2d 1473 (4th Cir. 2012) (holding that summary judgment was not appropriate because there was a genuine issue of material fact as to whether Google was causing consumer confusion by using trademark terms to trigger keyword advertising for parties other than the trademark owner);

[Delete the last sentence of the carry-over paragraph on page 391.]

[Replace the second through the last sentence in the full paragraph on page 391 with the following text.]

---

[17]No. 2:09-CV-990, 2012 U.S. Dist. LEXIS 27504 (D. Utah Mar. 1, 2012).
[18]*Id.*, 2012 U.S. Dist. LEXIS 27504, at *26 (emphasis in original).

Some courts have focused on the question of whether the defendant's sponsored links are likely to cause confusion, or to cause mistake, or to deceive as to the affiliation, connection, or association of the defendant's sponsored links.[19] But in *Rosetta Stone Ltd. v. Google, Inc.*,[20] the district court held that the relevant inquiry "is whether Google's practice of auctioning the [trademarks] as keyword triggers for Sponsored Links and allowing their use within Sponsored Links' text or title is likely to create confusion among consumers as to the source or origin of [the trademark owner's] goods or services"[21] and found on summary judgment that Google could not be liable for selling Rosetta Stone's trademarks because "there is no evidence that Google is attempting to pass off its goods or services as Rosetta Stone's."[22] On appeal, the Fourth Circuit reversed this holding, concluding instead that "there is sufficient evidence in the record to create a question of fact … to preclude summary judgment."[23] Importantly, the Fourth Circuit held that "[m]ore than just source confusion is at issue in an infringement claim" and specifically emphasized that confusion as to "'*sponsorship* of the goods'" can give rise to a claim under the Lanham Act.[24]

In determining whether confusion is likely, the Fourth Circuit emphasized that courts should continue to use the traditional likelihood-of-confusion multi-factor test and, in particular, to provide "at least a brief explanation of its reasons"[25] for concluding that certain factors are not relevant, even if "there is no hard and fast rule that obligates the district court to discuss each non-mandatory factor."[26] Accordingly, the onus remains on the trademark plaintiffs to show factually that an overall review of the traditional likelihood-of-confusion factors applied by courts supports their arguments as to confusion allegedly caused by the use of trademarks as keywords.

In applying this test, the Fourth Circuit found that the similarity of the marks at issue, the strength of the plaintiff's mark, the similarity of the parties' goods and services, the quality of the defendant's goods, the similarity of facilities, and the similarity of advertising were either "of limited value" or else not relevant in cases such as this where advertisers were allegedly making intentional "nominative" uses of the plaintiff's

---

[19] *See, e.g.*, Mary Kay, Inc. v. Weber, 661 F. Supp. 2d 632, 640 (N.D. Tex. 2009) (entering injunction because the defendant's use of trademarks as keywords "caused confusion about their affiliation with Mary Kay"); *see also* 15 U.S.C. §1125(a) (prohibiting use of a mark "likely to cause confusion, or to cause mistake, or to deceive as to the affiliation, connection, or association of [the defendant] with another person, or as to the origin, sponsorship, or approval of his or her goods, services, or commercial activities by another person").

[20] 730 F. Supp. 2d 531, 97 USPQ2d 1855 (E.D. Va. 2010). *Rosetta Stone* is also discussed in Sections VIII.B, X.I.2, and XVI.B.5 in this chapter of the supplement.

[21] *Rosetta Stone*, 730 F. Supp. 2d at 541, 97 USPQ2d at 1862.

[22] *Id.*, 97 USPQ2d at 1862 (E.D. Va. 2010).

[23] Rosetta Stone Ltd. v. Google, Inc., 676 F.3d 144, 160, 102 USPQ2d 1473, 1485 (4th Cir. 2012).

[24] *Id.* at 157, 102 USPQ2d at 1482 (quoting PETA v. Doughney, 263 F.3d 359, 366, 60 USPQ2d 1109, 1113 (4th Cir. 2001)) (emphasis added by the court).

[25] *Id.* at 155, 102 USPQ2d at 1481.

[26] *Id.* at 154, 102 USPQ2d at 1480.

mark to sell the plaintiff's own goods or competitive goods.[27] This creates something of a minor conflict with the Ninth Circuit, which found in the *Network Automation* case that the strength of the plaintiff's mark factor is first among "the most relevant factors" in keyword cases.[28] There is at least some logic to both positions. On one hand, if a mark is strong and famous, it is likely that consumers who search for the mark are seeking the owner of that mark and may be confused by the appearance of links to unaffiliated or unauthorized Web sites. On the other hand, if legitimate resellers are using a mark honestly to convey that they offer that brand of product, the question of liability may turn on other elements of a fair use analysis, regardless of the strength of the mark.

On the key question, the Fourth Circuit concluded that with respect to the remaining factors—Google's intent, actual confusion, and the sophistication of the relevant consuming public—Rosetta Stone had proffered enough evidence that a reasonable jury could reach a finding of infringement.[29]

In evaluating Google's intent, the Fourth Circuit reviewed evidence that Google had allegedly made a conscious decision to allow the use of trademark keywords in its search advertising program despite an awareness of "significant source confusion among Internet searchers" when trademarks were used in search advertising, out of a "largely financial" motive.[30] The court concluded "that a reasonable trier of fact *could* find that Google intended to cause confusion in that it acted with the knowledge that confusion was very likely to result from its use of the marks."[31]

In evaluating actual confusion, the Fourth Circuit reviewed "both survey and anecdotal evidence of actual confusion in connection with Google's use of trademarks in its AdWords program"[32] and again concluded that the evidence was sufficient to support a reasonable jury finding of liability. More specifically:

- The Fourth Circuit disagreed with the district court as to the significance of deposition testimony of five consumers who inadvertently bought counterfeit Rosetta Stone products via the Internet after Google began permitting use of Rosetta Stone trademarks in sponsored links. The district court had concluded that this testimony was "*de minimis* given that there were only five instances of actual confusion out of more than '100,000 impressions over

---

[27] *Id.* at 154–55, 102 USPQ2d at 1480–81; *see also* Section X in this supplement and in the main volume, *infra*.

[28] Network Automation, Inc. v. Advanced Sys. Concepts, Inc., 638 F.3d 1137, 1154, 97 USPQ2d 2036, 2047 (9th Cir. 2011) (the others being "(2) the evidence of actual confusion; (3) the type of goods and degree of care likely to be exercised by the purchaser; and (4) the labeling and appearance of the advertisements and the surrounding context on the screen displaying the results page").

[29] *Rosetta Stone*, 676 F.3d at 160, 102 USPQ2d at 1485.

[30] *Id.* at 155–56, 102 USPQ2d at 1481.

[31] *Id.* at 156, 102 USPQ2d at 1481 (emphasis in original).

[32] *Id.*, 102 USPQ2d at 1481–82.

six years.'"[33] Although the Fourth Circuit agreed that a *de minimis* number of consumer complaints may be dismissed "where the number of opportunities for confusion is great,"[34] in this instance, the deposition testimony was supplemented by evidence that Rosetta Stone had received 123 unsolicited customer complaints from consumers who bought counterfeits thinking them to be genuine. "Although this evidence does not indicate whether each customer logging a complaint made the purchase via a sponsored link, it is reasonable, for purposes of summary judgment, to infer that a great number of these individuals were confused by the apparent relationship between Rosetta Stone and the sponsored link ...."[35]

- The Fourth Circuit also reviewed evidence of "various in-house studies conducted by Google 'to analyze user confusion (if any) associated with ads using [trademark] terms,'" including one study of reactions to sponsored links with a trademark in the text or title which concluded that "94% of users were confused at least once." The Court of Appeals concluded that this evidence was "probative as to actual confusion in connection with Google's use of trademarks."[36]

- Additionally, the Fourth Circuit pointed to the testimony of two in-house Google trademark attorneys who were shown a Google search results page for the keyword phrase "Rosetta Stone," and were "unable to determine without more research which sponsored links were authorized resellers of ROSETTA STONE products." According to the Court of Appeals, the "district court should have accepted it as evidence of actual confusion for summary judgment purposes; whether it is entitled to enough weight to carry the day on the ultimate issue is a matter for trial."[37]

- Finally, the Fourth Circuit reviewed the consumer confusion survey report of Dr. Kent Van Liere showing a 17 percent net confusion rate, which the court called "clear evidence of actual confusion for purposes of summary judgment."[38] The survey showed consumers

---

[33] *Id.* at 157–58, 102 USPQ2d at 1483 (quoting *Rosetta Stone*, 730 F. Supp. 2d at 543, 97 USPQ2d at 1863). The Fourth Circuit also rejected the district court's view that these examples of actual confusion were irrelevant because none of the sponsored links at issue conformed to Google's internal policies: "Whether the sponsored link conforms to Google's policy is not an issue that bears upon whether the consuming public, which is not privy to these policies, is confused by the *actual* use of the trademarks in sponsored links. What matters is whether 'the defendant's *actual practice* is likely to produce confusion in the minds of consumers about the origin of the goods or services in question.'" *Id.* at 157, 102 USPQ2d at 1483 (quoting CareFirst of Md., Inc. v. First Care, P.C., 434 F.3d 263, 267, 77 USPQ2d 1577, 1579 (4th Cir. 2006)) (emphasis in original, emphasis in quoted material added by the court).

[34] *Id.* at 158, 102 USPQ2d at 1483 (citing George & Co., LLC v. Imagination Entm't Ltd., 575 F.3d 383, 398, 91 USPQ2d 1786, 1794 (4th Cir. 2009)).

[35] *Id.*, 102 USPQ2d at 1483.

[36] *Id.*, 102 USPQ2d at 1483.

[37] *Id.* 158, 159, 102 USPQ2d at 1483, 1483–84.

[38] *Id.* at 159, 102 USPQ2d at 1484.

a Google results page generated by the search term "Rosetta Stone," and asked them first, "Which link or links if any do you think sells Rosetta Stone language software products?"; "Of the links you just mentioned, which link or links if any, are a Rosetta Stone company website?"; and then "Of the links you mentioned, which link or links, if any, are endorsed by the Rosetta Stone company?"

In evaluating the sophistication of the relevant consuming public, the Fourth Circuit rejected the district court's finding that the relevant market of potential purchasers "'is comprised of well-educated consumers' who 'are more likely to spend time searching and learning about Rosetta Stone's products.'"[39] Based on some of the same evidence discussed in terms of "actual confusion," the Court of Appeals concluded that "there is sufficient evidence in the record to create a question of fact as to consumer sophistication that cannot be resolved on summary judgment."[40]

After the Fourth Circuit remanded the case back to the district court, Rosetta Stone and Google entered into a settlement that resulted in a dismissal of the action before the case could be tried. Although the terms of the settlement were confidential, Rosetta Stone general counsel Michael C. Wu was quoted as saying that he was very pleased with this settlement, that it was "a significant victory for consumer protection, and it goes a long way toward advancing our goal to strengthen the Rosetta Stone brand and trademarks around the world." As a result, it remains for future cases to clarify further whether the sale of trademarks as keywords constitutes trademark infringement.

[Revise the Section IX.C.4 heading to read as follows.]

4.   *Liability for "Broad Match" Advertisements [Revised Heading]*

X. Nominative Fair Use and The Internet

I.   Post-*Century 21* Nominative Fair Use Developments

[Add the following new section.]

2.   *The Fourth Circuit Defers Accepting or Rejecting the Nominative Fair Use Defense [New Topic]*

District courts in the Fourth Circuit have declined adopting either the Third or Ninth Circuit standard for nominative fair use.[41]

---

[39] *Id.*, 102 USPQ2d at 1484 (quoting *Rosetta Stone*, 730 F. Supp. 2d at 545, 92 USPQ2d at 1865).

[40] *Id.* at 160, 102 USPQ2d at 1484–85.

[41] *See, e.g.*, Lorillard Tobacco Co. v. S&M Brands, Inc., 616 F. Supp. 2d 581, 588, 589 (E.D. Va. 2009) (describing nominative fair use as a "common law defense asserted against alleged trademark infringement—though not used in [the Fourth Circuit]" and recognizing that the

In April 2012, the Fourth Circuit Court of Appeals issued its long-awaited decision in *Rosetta Stone Ltd. v. Google, Inc.*[42] In this case, the circuit court had an opportunity to adopt a nominative fair use standard for courts in the Fourth Circuit, but ultimately declined to do so. Instead, the *Rosetta Stone* court focused on other issues addressed in the district court's decision below, and left open the questions of whether on remand: (a) the district court should consider a nominative fair use test, and (b) if so, which version of the nominative fair use test should be used.

This case involved claims that Google had directly and secondarily infringed the plaintiff's mark by selling the mark "Rosetta Stone" as a key word for Internet searches. The trial court had granted Google summary judgment on a variety of grounds but did not discuss the nominative fair use defense at all. On the trademark infringement claim, the Fourth Circuit defended the district court's decision to address only three of the traditional likelihood-of-confusion factors (intent, actual confusion, and consumer sophistication), stating that "there is no hard and fast rule that obligates the district court to discuss each non-mandatory factor."[43] Although the court could have rested on well-established case law concluding that the multi-factor test is not exhaustive, it instead explained that when a challenged use of a trademark by a third party is referential or nominative in nature, then application of the traditional multi-factor test is difficult because often a number of the factors are of little probative value.[44] The Court of Appeals, however, expressly declined to set forth the standards of a normative fair use defense, stating:

> We hasten to add that we are not adopting a position about the viability of the nominative fair-use doctrine as a defense to trademark infringement or whether this doctrine should formally alter our likelihood-of-confusion test in some way. That question has not been presented here and we leave it for another day. We have merely attempted to highlight the problems inherent in the robotic application of each and every factor in a case involving a referential, nontrademark use. Accordingly, the district court did not commit reversible error in failing to address every factor [of the likelihood-of-confusion test]. In the future, however, a district court opting not to address a given factor or group of factors should provide at least a brief explanation of its reasons.[45]

The Fourth Circuit may have been signaling to the district court that the lower court may want to consider an alternative to the traditional multi-factor likelihood-of-confusion test as *Rosetta Stone* progresses on remand. Only time will tell.

Fourth Circuit has not adopted the nominative fair use standard "in any form"); National Fed'n of the Blind v. Loompanics Enters., 936 F. Supp. 1232, 1241 (D. Md. 1996) (Blake, J.) ("Because the *New Kids* test is not the law of [the Fourth] Circuit, and because neither the [Lanham Act] nor Fourth Circuit case law portend its adoption, I decline to follow it.").

[42] Rosetta Stone Ltd. v. Google, Inc., 676 F.3d 144, 102 USPQ2d 1473 (4th Cir. 2012). *Rosetta Stone* is also discussed in Sections VIII.B, IX.C.2, and XVI.B.5 in this chapter of the supplement.

[43] *Rosetta Stone*, 676 F.3d at 154, 102 USPQ2d at 1480.

[44] *Id.* at 153–55, 102 USPQ2d at 1479–81.

[45] *Id.* at 155, 102 USPQ2d at 1481.

The *Rosetta Stone* decision also raised the nominative fair use defense in connection with its reversal of the district court's decision to dispose of Rosetta Stone's trademark dilution claim. The district court had required that Rosetta Stone prove in its prima facie dilution claim that Google was using the Rosetta Stone mark as a source identifier for *Google's* own products and that "use of the mark was likely to impair the distinctiveness of or harm the reputation of the ROSETTA STONE marks."[46] The Fourth Circuit held that the district court essentially misread the statutory "fair use" defense in the FTDA[47] to mean that if the defendant is not using the plaintiff's mark as a source identifier for the defendant's goods, then the plaintiff has failed to establish a prima facie claim for dilution. The Fourth Circuit clarified that the burden of showing that Google was or was not making a fair use of the Rosetta Stone mark is squarely on Google, once Rosetta Stone established its prima facie case that Google's use of the marks was likely to blur or tarnish the Rosetta Stone marks.[48]

Again, the Fourth Circuit declined to go on record adopting any particular formulation of the nominative fair use test. Notably, the Fourth Circuit referenced both the Ninth Circuit's *New Kids* definition of nominative fair use and the Fifth Circuit *Smack Apparel* test,[49] and stated that whichever type of fair use is claimed by the dilution defendant, the fair use defense must include an element of "good faith,"[50] that is, that the accused infringer did not intend "'to create consumer confusion as to source *or sponsorship.*'"[51] By deferring adoption of a specific nominative fair use standard in the Fourth Circuit, the court leaves it to the parties and the district court to divine which standard should be used on remand as a statutory defense to Rosetta Stone's FTDA claim. As a result, litigants in the Fourth Circuit may continue to be required to rely on the traditional likelihood-of-confusion test, and as a contingency look to the tests of the other circuits until this defense's viability and contours are settled in the Fourth Circuit.

[Redesignate Section X.I.2 as Section X.I.3 as follows.]

---

[46] *Id.* at 168, 102 USPQ2d at 1490–91.

[47] *See* 15 U.S.C. §1125(c)(3)(A) (the statutory "fair use" defense protects a party's "fair use" of a plaintiff's mark as long as such use is not as "a designation of source for the [defendant's] own goods or services").

[48] *Rosetta Stone*, 676 F.3d at 168–69, 102 USPQ2d at 1491. On the issue of blurring, the court noted that even where evidence indicates that public recognition of the defendants' product increased, a court must consider other dilution factors and must focus its inquiry not on actual injury but on the "*likelihood* of dilution." *Id.* at 170–71, 102 USPQ2d at 1493 (emphasis in original).

[49] *Id.* at 169–70, 102 USPQ2d at 1492 (citing New Kids on the Block v. News America Pub., Inc., 971 F.2d 302, 308, 23 USPQ2d 1534, 1538 (9th Cir. 1992); Board of Supervisors v. Smack Apparel Co., 550 F.3d 465, 489, 89 USPQ2d 1338, 1352–53 (5th Cir. 2008)).

[50] *Id.* at 169, 102 USPQ2d at 1492 (citing JA Apparel Corp. v. Abboud, 568 F.3d 390, 401, 91 USPQ2d 1095, 1102–03 (2d Cir. 2009); Sands, Taylor & Wood Co. v. Quaker Oats Co., 978 F.2d 947, 951, 24 USPQ2d 1001, 1005 (7th Cir. 1992)).

[51] *Id.*, 102 USPQ2d at 1492 (quoting *JA Apparel*, 568 F.3d at 401, 91 USPQ2d 1103) (emphasis added by the court).

3.   The Second Circuit Refuses to Adopt Either the Third or Ninth Circuit Analysis [Redesignated]

[In the first line of the first paragraph of redesignated Section X.I.3 on page 414, replace "Most recently, in" with "In."]

[Redesignate Section X.I.3 as Section X.I.4 as follows.]

4.   The Latest from the Ninth Circuit [Redesignated]

[708a][Add the following new footnote 708a at the end of the first full sentence of the carry-over paragraph on page 417.] One court, however, has granted a motion to dismiss in relying on the nominative fair use defense raised by Judge Alex Kozinski's *Tabari* opinion. In *Architectural Mailboxes LLC v. Epoch Design LLC*, No. 10cv974, 2011 U.S. Dist. LEXIS 46180, 99 USPQ2d 1799 (S.D. Cal. Apr. 28, 2011), the plaintiff unknowingly contributed to this result by attaching the allegedly infringing advertisements and Web pages to the complaint. The court noted that the site specifically states that the mark in question is a registered mark of the plaintiff. More importantly, however, the court emphasized that "every statement" about the plaintiff's product was negative, providing no basis for concluding that the defendant was attempting to suggest that it was sponsored by or affiliated with the plaintiff. *Id.*, 2011 U.S. Dist. LEXIS 46180, at *8, 99 USPQ2d at 1802.

XI. FREE SPEECH AND PARODY ISSUES

B.   Gripe Sites

[731][Add the following text to footnote 731 after the *Taubman* citation and parenthetical note.] ; Ascentive, LLC v. Opinion Corp., No. 10 Civ. 4433, WL 6181452, *9, 2011 U.S. Dist. LEXIS 143081, at *34–36 (E.D.N.Y. Dec. 13, 2011) (consumers were unlikely to believe Web sites at PissedConsumer.com, which allowed users to create domain names incorporating brands they wished to criticize, such as Ascentive.PissedConsumer.com to criticize Ascentive, were official or sponsored sites because of the use of "pissed" in the domain name as well as the critical content of the sites);

XII. USE OF DISCLAIMERS ONLINE

B.   Effective Disclaimers

[755a][Add the following new footnote 755a after the first sentence of the first paragraph of Section XII.B on page 425.] *See, e.g.*, TrafficSchool. com, Inc. v. Edriver, Inc., 653 F.3d 820, 829, 99 USPQ2d 1628, 1635 (9th Cir. 2011) (holding that district court did not abuse its discretion when

it concluded that an injunction requiring a splash screen disclaimer to be presented to every site visitor was the optimal means of correcting the defendants' false advertising).

XV. COUNTERFEITING AND THE INTERNET

A. Civil Litigation

1. *Personal Jurisdiction*

[Revise the Section XV.A.1.a heading to read as follows.]

    a.   Interactive Web Sites Selling Goods in the Forum [Revised Heading]

[Revise the Section XV.A.1.b heading to read as follows.]

    b.   Providing Services to Interactive Web Site Selling Counterfeit Goods in the Forum [Revised Heading]

    c.   Injury to Mark Holder in Forum

[830][Add the following text at the end of footnote 830.] In *Troma Entm't, Inc. v. Centennial Pictures Inc.*, No. 11 Civ. 1137, 2012 WL 1178998, 2012 U.S. Dist. LEXIS 50430 (E.D.N.Y. Apr. 10, 2012), the court emphasized that infringement on the Internet—where the copyrighted works were available to New Yorkers—was key to the court's holding in *Penguin Group*: "What *Penguin Group* was concerned with was not just copyrights, but the use of the internet to sell or exhibit purloined copyrighted material to anyone, including potential New York buyers." *Id.* at *3, 2012 U.S. Dist. LEXIS 50430, at *7. In *Troma*, though, the court declined to find jurisdiction over the defendant, a California resident who had provided copyright-protected films to a German company, because the New York plaintiff's works were not disseminated online or otherwise made available to New York customers. *Id.* at *4, 2012 U.S. Dist. LEXIS 50430, at *9–10.

2. *Post-Sale Confusion*

[837][Add the following text at the end of footnote 837.] The Second Circuit recently reaffirmed the post-sale confusion standard in *Louis Vuitton Malletier S.A. v. Ly USA, Inc.*, 2012 WL 1034540, at *2, 2012 U.S. App. LEXIS 6517, at *4–5, 102 USPQ2d 1249 (2d Cir. Mar. 29, 2012) ("The likelihood that the use of plaintiff's marks would lead individuals other than purchasers of the knockoff products to believe that they were manufactured by the trademark-holder (so-called 'post-sale confusion') provides further support for the judgment of the district court.") (citing

Hermès Int'l v. Lederer de Paris Fifth Ave., Inc., 219 F.3d 104, 108–09, 55 USPQ2d 1360, 1364 (2d Cir. 2000)).

3.   Ex Parte *Injunctive Relief*

a.   *Asset Freeze*

[851] [Add the following text at the end of footnote 851.] After the court in *Li* denied the non-party bank's motion to modify the preliminary injunction with respect to assets maintained abroad, the bank moved for reconsideration on the basis of a letter from Chinese bank regulators to the court setting forth their objection to the bank's production of documents from China. The court denied the bank's motion for reconsideration, finding that the letter from the Chinese regulators would not have altered the original outcome. Memorandum and Order, Gucci Am., Inc. v. Li, No. 10 Civ. 4974, 2012 U.S. Dist. LEXIS 72650, at *8, *13–15, 2012 WL 1883352, at *4–5 (S.D.N.Y. May 18, 2012).

[Add the following text at the end of the carry-over paragraph on page 442.]

Another recent decision of the Southern District of New York confirmed the court's equitable power to freeze the defendants' assets, including assets maintained in China, to preserve the plaintiffs' equitable right to an accounting and return of the counterfeiters' profits under the Lanham Act.[52]

b.   *Expedited Discovery*

[856] [Add the following text at the end of footnote 856.] *But see* Tiffany (NJ) LLC v. Qi Andrew, 276 F.R.D. 143, 2011 U.S. Dist. LEXIS 80677 (S.D.N.Y. July 25, 2011). In *Qi Andrew*, the court ruled that the plaintiffs should first attempt to obtain discovery of the defendants' bank records maintained by three non-party banks in China through the Hague Convention in deference to Chinese bank secrecy law, but stated that the court would reconsider compelling the banks to produce the documents if the Hague Convention process proved futile. *Id.* at 160–61, 2011 U.S. Dist. LEXIS 80677, at *57–58. A subsequent district court reviewed what was ultimately produced in response to the *Qi Andrew* Hague Convention request over a year after the *Qi Andrew* decision, and concluded that "the Chinese Ministry of Justice's response ... denied some of the valid discovery requested by the court's Letter of Request." Wultz v. Bank of China, 11 Civ. 1266 (SAS) (S.D.N.Y. Oct. 29, 2012) (slip op.).

The court in *Forbse* took the middle ground, ordering the plaintiffs to seek discovery from two of three Chinese banks via the Hague Conven-

---

[52] Memorandum and Order, Tiffany (NJ) LLC v. Forbse, No. 11 Civ. 4976, 2012 U.S. Dist. LEXIS 72148 (S.D.N.Y. May 23, 2012), at 30–31.

tion but requiring the Bank of China to produce documents pursuant to the expedited discovery provisions of the preliminary injunction entered by the court. Memorandum and Order, Tiffany (NJ) LLC v. Forbse, No. 11 Civ. 4976, 2012 U.S. Dist. LEXIS 72148, at *20–21 (S.D.N.Y. May 23, 2012).

4. Defenses to Trademark Counterfeiting

b. Parody

[867][Add the following text at the end of footnote 867.] A "subtle satire" of the original mark, as opposed to an "over-the-top" parody, does not constitute a fair use defense to trademark dilution. Louis Vuitton Malletier, S.A. v. Hyundai Motor Am., No. 10 Civ. 1611, 2012 WL 102247, 2012 U.S. Dist. LEXIS 42795 (S.D.N.Y. Mar. 22, 2012).

5. Statutory Damages

[871][Add the following text at the end of footnote 871.] Courts increasingly award high statutory damages for online counterfeiting. In 2012, a district court awarded statutory damages of $100 million in a case involving thirty-four infringing Web sites that offered for sale at least nine types of goods bearing Hermès trademarks. Default Judgment and Permanent Injunction, Hermès Int'l v. Doe, No. 12 Civ. 1623 (S.D.N.Y. Apr. 30, 2012) (see Bloomberg.com, Hermes Wins $100 Million Damages From Counterfeit Websites, available at http://www.bloomberg.com/news/2012-04-30/hermes-wins-100-million-in-damages-from-websites-selling-fakes.html). Another court awarded $200,000 per mark infringed for a total of $12.4 million. Default Judgment, Balenciaga Am., Inc. v. Dollinger, No. 10 Civ. 2912 (S.D.N.Y. Jan. 3, 2012).

B. Government Enforcement

[873][Replace the text of footnote 873 with the following.] U.S. Immigrations and Customs Enforcement News Release, Special Agents and Officers Seize more than $4.8 Million in Fake NFL Merchandise and Seize 307 Websites During 'Operation Fake Sweep,' (Feb. 2, 2012), available at http://www.iprcenter.gov/partners/ice/news-releases/special-agents-and-officers-seize-more-than-4.8-million-in-fake-nfl-merchandise-and-seize-307-websites-during-operation-fake-sweep (last visited May 23, 2012).

[874][Replace the text of footnote 874 with the following.]

Since the fall of 2010, the government has deployed this initiative to seize hundreds of Web sites offering either pirated movies and music or counterfeit hard goods.

[Add the following text after the carry-over paragraph on page 446.]

The government has recently used a provision of the Patriot Act to seize proceeds of counterfeit sales deposited in accounts overseas. After criminal investigation of a counterfeiting operation revealed that counterfeiters used PayPal to process payments for counterfeit goods and then wired the proceeds to bank accounts in China, the government obtained warrants to seize $826,883 from correspondent accounts held by the Chinese banks in the United States.[53]

XVI. SECONDARY TRADEMARK LIABILITY

A. Origins of Secondary Liability for Trademark Infringement

1. Inwood *and Its Progeny*

  b.   Inwood *Applied to Brick and Mortar Service Providers*

[Add the following text after the third sentence of the second paragraph on page 448.]

To meet the "knowledge" prong of the test, the plaintiffs must show that the defendants had actual knowledge or constructive knowledge of the underlying infringement, *i.e.*, that the defendant *should* have known about the direct infringement.[54] The plaintiff does not need to show that the contributor infringer acted intentionally,[55] and, in fact, ignorance may not be a defense to a contributory infringement claim.[56]

[890][Add the following text at the beginning of footnote 890.] *See, e.g.*, Rosetta Stone, Ltd. v. Google, Inc., 676 F.3d 144, 165, 102 USPQ2d 1473, 1488 (4th Cir. 2012) ("[L]iability for vicarious trademark infringement requires 'a finding that the defendant and the infringer have an apparent or actual partnership, have authority to bind one another in transactions with third parties or exercise joint ownership or control over the infringing product.'") (quoting Hard Rock Café Licensing Corp. v. Concession Servs., Inc., 955 F.2d 1143, 1150, 21 USPQ2d 1764, 1769 (7th Cir. 1992));

---

[53]Immigrations and Customs Enforcement News Release, More than $896,000 in Proceeds Seized from the Online Sale of Counterfeit Sports Apparel Manufactured in China, Apr. 10, 2012, *available at* http://www.iprcenter.gov/partners/ice/news-releases/more-than-896-000-in-proceeds-seized-from-the-online-sale-of-counterfeit-sports-apparel-manufactured-in-china (last visited May 23, 2012); Verified Complaint for Forfeiture In Rem, U.S. v. All Funds in Indus. and Commercial Bank of China Ltd. Interbank Accounts in the Unites States, No. 1:12 cv 00489 (D.D.C. Mar. 22, 2012).

[54]Louis Vuitton Malletier, S.A. v. Akanoc Solutions, Inc., 658 F.3d 936, 943, 100 USPQ2d 1124, 1129 (9th Cir. 2011).

[55]*Id.*, 100 USPQ2d at 1129.

[56]Roger Cleveland Golf Co. v. Prince, No. 2:09-CV-2119, 2012 WL 1106775, at *4, 2012 U.S. Dist. LEXIS 46065, at *27 (D.S.C. Mar. 30, 2012).

[891][Replace the text of footnote 891 with the following.] 955 F.2d at 1149, 21 USPQ2d at 1768.

B.   Secondary Liability in the Online Context

[900][In footnote 900, replace the *Rosetta Stone* citation and parenthetical note with the following.] Rosetta Stone Ltd. v. Google, Inc., 676 F.3d 144, 165, 102 USPQ2d 1473, 1488 (4th Cir. 2012) (affirming district court's grant of summary judgment on vicarious infringement claim where there was no evidence that Google acted jointly with third-party advertisers to control the counterfeit Rosetta Stone products);

[Also in footnote 900, add the following text at the end of the footnote.]

Car-Freshner Corp. v. Getty Images, Inc., 822 F. Supp. 2d 167 (N.D.N.Y. 2011) (granting motion to dismiss vicarious infringement claim concerning infringing photographs on the defendants' Web site).

2.   *Credit Card Processors*

[907][Add the following text at the end of footnote 907.]; http:// www.mastercard.com/us/company/en/docs/Anatomy_of_a_Transaction_030212.pdf.

3.   *Internet Service Providers ("ISPs")*

b.   Louis Vuitton Malletier, S.A. v. Akanoc Solutions, Inc.

[Replace the first three paragraphs of the section with the following text.]

Luxury goods retailer Louis Vuitton brought suit against Akanoc Solutions, Inc., Managed Solutions Group, Inc. ("MSG") and Steven Chen, who managed Akanoc and MSG, based on their roles in hosting Web sites selling infringing Louis Vuitton products.[57] Louis Vuitton alleged that the defendants were contributorily liable for the Web sites' infringement because they failed to take appropriate action after being provided with notice of specific Web sites selling counterfeit products. The district court denied the defendants' motion for summary judgment on contributory trademark infringement, finding that there were genuine issues of material fact regarding their knowledge of the underlying infringement and their extent of control over the infringing Web sites.

---

[57]Louis Vuitton Malletier, S.A. v. Akanoc Solutions, Inc., 591 F. Supp. 2d 1098 (N.D. Cal. 2008), *aff'd in part, rev'd in part*, 658 F.3d 936, 100 USPQ2d 1124 (9th Cir. 2011).

In denying the defendants' motion, the district court noted that "Defendants physically host websites on their servers and route internet traffic to and from those websites. This service is the internet equivalent of leasing real estate.… As with the flea market operators in *Fonovisa*, Defendants cannot remain 'willfully blind' to trademark infringement taking place on their servers."[58] The court did, however, grant the defendants' summary judgment on Louis Vuitton's claim for vicarious infringement.

At trial, a jury found Akanoc, MSG, and Chen liable for willful contributory trademark infringement of thirteen trademarks and awarded Louis Vuitton $10.5 million in statutory damages against each defendant, for a total of $31.5 million in statutory damages.[59] The district court subsequently rejected the defendants' attempt to set aside the award as unconstitutionally punitive.[60] The district court also denied the defendants' post-trial motions for judgment as a matter of law except with respect to defendant MSG.[61] As to MSG, the court concluded that "there was no evidence indicating that MSG … did anything more than own and lease the hardware operated by Akanoc and Chen."[62] On appeal, the Ninth Circuit largely affirmed the district court's handling of the case, but found that the defendants could only be held liable for one single, joint and several statutory damages award, not three duplicative statutory damages awards.[63]

c.   Roger Cleveland Golf Company v. Prince

[Replace all of the text of the section with the following text.]

In *Roger Cleveland Golf Co. v. Prince*,[64] a golf equipment company alleged that the company that hosted and designed an infringing Web site

---

[58] *Id.*, 591 F. Supp. 2d at 1112. By contrast, in *Lockheed Martin*, the Ninth Circuit rejected the argument that Network Solutions' registrar service was analogous to the provision of real estate, finding that "[i]n *Fonovisa* and *Hard Rock* … the defendants licensed real estate, with the consequent direct control over the activity that the third-party alleged infringers engaged in on the premises." Lockheed Martin Corp. v. Network Solutions, Inc., 194 F.3d 980, 985, 52 USPQ2d 1481, 1485 (9th Cir. 1999). Instead, the Ninth Circuit described Network Solutions' role as "differ[ing] little from that of the United States Postal Service.… NSI does not supply the domain-name combination any more than the Postal Service supplies a street address by performing the routine service of routing mail." *Id.* at 984–85, 52 USPQ2d at 1484.

[59] *Akanoc*, 658 F.3d at 941, 100 USPQ2d at 1128. The jury also awarded $300,000 in statutory damages against each defendant for willful copyright infringement of the two copyrights.

[60] *See* Louis Vuitton Malletier, S.A. v. Akanoc Solutions, Inc., No. C 07-03952, 2010 WL 5598337, 2010 U.S. Dist. LEXIS 85266, 97 USPQ2d 1178 (N.D. Cal. Mar. 19, 2010).

[61] *Akanoc*, 658 F.3d at 941, 100 USPQ2d at 1128.

[62] *Id.*, 100 USPQ2d at 1128. The court affirmed the district court's grant of judgment as a matter of law to MSG. *Id.* at 942, 100 USPQ2d at 1128.

[63] *Id.* at 946–47, 100 USPQ2d at 1132–33.

[64] No. 2:09-CV-2119, 2010 WL 5019260, 2010 U.S. Dist. LEXIS 128044 (D.S.C. Dec. 3, 2010), *motion denied*, No. 2:09-CV-2119, 2012 WL 1106775, 2012 U.S. Dist. LEXIS 46065 (D.S.C. Mar. 30, 2012).

was contributorily liable for infringement. The District of South Carolina denied that company's motion for summary judgment, rejecting the
argument that it only functioned as a Web site host.[65] The plaintiff had
offered evidence that defendant Bright Builders was not just a host, but
meaningfully participated in the creation of and development of the Web
site and business model, including recommending that the infringer use
"wholesalers" and "drop shippers" to fulfill customer orders.[66] The plaintiff also proffered evidence that the company knew or should have known
that its customer was selling counterfeit golf clubs, and that the name of
the Web site, copycatclubs.com, should have put the defendant on notice
of its client's intent to infringe.[67]

After a two-day jury trial, Bright Builders was found liable for willful
contributory trademark infringement, and the jury awarded the plaintiff $770,000 in statutory damages under the Lanham Act, representing
$70,000 per mark infringed.[68] In contrast, the direct infringer was found
liable for $2,500 per mark in statutory damages.[69] The court rejected
Bright Builders' post-trial motions seeking relief from the judgment and
a new trial, including Bright Builders' motion for remittitur. The court
concluded that the jury award was not excessive even if the jury awarded
greater damages based on Bright Builders' conduct as a contributory infringer than it did for the direct infringement.[70] The court found that
the jury's award was well within the statutory range, noting that the jury's
award of $70,000 per mark infringed was only a fraction of the $2,000,000
maximum per mark permitted under the Lanham Act.[71]

4. Virtual World Infringement

[Replace the second sentence of the first paragraph of the section on
page 457 with the following text, retaining footnote 945.]

An illustrative case was brought in the Northern District of California
alleging the unauthorized use of trademarks in an online virtual world.

[Replace the first sentence of the second paragraph of the section on
page 457 with the following text.]

In *Eros, LLC v. Linden Research, Inc.*, the plaintiffs filed a class action
against the owners and operators of the Internet-based interactive computer simulation "Second Life," an adults-only online virtual world where
users can, among other things, buy virtual versions of items that are protected by trademark and copyright.

---

[65] *Id.*, 2012 WL 1106775, at *1, 2012 U.S. Dist. LEXIS 46065, at *4.
[66] *Id.*, 2012 U.S. Dist. LEXIS 46065, at *3.
[67] *Id.*, 2012 U.S. Dist. LEXIS 46065, at *3.
[68] *Id.* at *5–6, 2012 U.S. Dist. LEXIS 46065, at *15–16.
[69] *Id.* at *10, 2012 U.S. Dist. LEXIS 46065, at *30.
[70] *Id.* at *10–11, 2012 U.S. Dist. LEXIS 46065, at *30.
[71] *Id.*, 2012 U.S. Dist. LEXIS 46065, at *31.

[Replace the last sentence of the second paragraph of the section on page 457 with the following text.]

Following a mediation between the parties, and before the court rendered any opinions in the action, the plaintiffs voluntarily withdrew their claims.[72] This leaves open the question of whether a court would treat the operators of a simulated environment as "landlords" for purposes of imposing secondary liability for infringement.

[Add the following new section.]

5. Search Engine Keyword Advertising [New Topic]

Plaintiffs have also sought to impose secondary liability on search engines that sell the plaintiffs' trademarked keywords to third-party advertisers. Although courts have been willing to uphold claims of contributory infringement in response to motions to dismiss or motions for summary judgment, it is often in the context where the court is required to resolve all inferences in favor of the trademark owner as the nonmoving party.[73] While the courts are willing to allow such claims to proceed, it remains to be seen whether any search engines will ultimately be held liable under theories of secondary liability.

In *Rosetta Stone, Ltd. v. Google, Inc.*,[74] the plaintiff asserted, among other things, that Google was contributorily and vicariously liable for trademark infringement based on Google's sale of the ROSETTA STONE trademark to third-party advertisers selling counterfeit versions of the Rosetta Stone language learning system.[75] Among other things, Rosetta Stone alleged that Google's Query Suggestion Tool, which recommended keywords to advertisers (including brand names), induced purchasers to commit trademark infringement.[76] Rosetta Stone also alleged that Google was also liable under the "extent of control" theory because it allowed counterfeiters to

---

[72] *See* Docket Entry Nos. 43–48, Eros, LLC v. Linden Research, Inc., No. CV 09 4269 (N.D. Cal.).

[73] *See, e.g.*, Rosetta Stone Ltd. v. Google, Inc., 676 F.3d 144, 165, 102 USPQ2d 1473, 1488 (4th Cir. 2012) (vacating district court's grant of summary judgment to Google on the plaintiffs' contributory infringement claim and remanding for further proceedings); Google, Inc. v. American Blind & Wallpaper Factory, Inc., No. C 03-05340, 2005 WL 832398, 2005 U.S. Dist. LEXIS 6228, 74 USPQ2d 1385 (N.D. Cal. Mar. 30, 2005) (denying Google's motion to dismiss counterclaim for contributory trademark infringement); American Airlines, Inc. v. Google, Inc., No. 4:07-CV-487-A (N.D. Tex. Oct. 24, 2007) (denying Google's motion to dismiss American Airline's suit over keyword advertising sales).

[74] 730 F. Supp. 2d 531, 97 USPQ2d 1855 (E.D. Va. 2010), *aff'd in part, rev'd in part*, 676 F.3d 144, 102 USPQ2d 1473 (4th Cir. 2012) (remanding for further proceedings on the plaintiff's claims for direct infringement, contributory infringement and dilution). *Rosetta Stone* is also discussed in Sections VIII.B, IX.C.2, and X.I.2 in this chapter of the supplement.

[75] *Rosetta Stone*, 730 F. Supp. 2d at 534–35, 97 USPQ2d at 1857.

[76] *Id.* at 547, 97 USPQ2d at 1866–67.

open AdWords accounts and bid on the Rosetta Stone trademarks despite receiving notice of their counterfeit status.[77]

To support its assertion that Google had knowledge of the ongoing infringement, Rosetta Stone pointed to a statement to the Securities and Exchange Commission, in which Google acknowledged that its Query Suggestion Tool might subject it to more trademark infringement lawsuits.[78] Rosetta Stone also provided evidence that it had notified Google of approximately 200 instances of Sponsored Links advertising counterfeit Rosetta Stone products over the course of a five-month period.[79]

Nevertheless, the court granted summary judgment in Google's favor. Relying on the Second Circuit's decision in *Tiffany*, the court found that "[l]ike Tiffany, Rosetta Stone fails to show that Google knew of the alleged infringing activity by its AdWords advertisers," and noted the steps Google has taken to assist law enforcement and brand owners in combating counterfeiting.[80] Although the court acknowledged that Google had implemented the tool with a "desire for economic gain," it found that such a desire "alone does not translate into contributory trademark infringement."[81] The court also rejected Rosetta Stone's claim for vicarious infringement, finding that Google lacked the requisite control over third-party advertisers.[82]

In April 2012, the Fourth Circuit vacated the district court's order granting summary judgment to Google on the contributory infringement claim and affirmed summary judgment on the vicarious infringement claim.[83] The Fourth Circuit found that "the district court turned the summary judgment standard on its head" in placing the burden on Rosetta Stone, the nonmoving party, to show that summary judgment was not proper.[84] The Fourth Circuit also rejected the district court's heavy reliance on the Second Circuit's decision in *Tiffany*, finding that the decision was "of limited application in these circumstances" because "the *Tiffany* court did not view the evidence through the lens of summary judgment."[85] Rather, the evidence in *Tiffany* was presented at a bench trial where the

---

[77] *Id.*, 97 USPQ2d at 1866–67.

[78] *Id.*, 97 USPQ2d at 1866–67.

[79] *Id.*, 97 USPQ2d at 1867.

[80] *Id.* at 548, 97 USPQ2d at 1867.

[81] *Id.*, 97 USPQ2d at 1867.

[82] *Id.* at 549, 97 USPQ2d at 1868 ("Absent an agency relationship, vicarious liability can only be imposed if the defendant and infringer 'exercise joint ownership or control over the infringing product.'") (quoting Perfect 10, Inc. v. Visa Int'l Serv. Ass'n, 494 F.3d 788, 807, 83 USPQ2d 1144, 1157 (9th Cir. 2007)); *but see* GEICO v. Google, Inc., 330 F. Supp. 2d 700, 705, 73 USPQ2d 1212, 1215 (E.D. Va. 2004) (finding that GEICO sufficiently stated a claim for vicarious infringement).

[83] *Rosetta Stone*, 676 F.3d at 149–50, 102 USPQ2d at 1476.

[84] 676 F.3d at 164, 102 USPQ2d at 1488. "While it may very well be that Rosetta Stone was not entitled to summary judgment, that issue is not before us. The only question … is whether, viewing the evidence and drawing all reasonable inferences from that evidence in a light most favorable to Rosetta Stone, a reasonable trier of fact could find in favor of Rosetta Stone, the nonmoving party." *Id.* at 164–65, 102 USPQ2d at 1488.

[85] *Id.* at 165, 102 USPQ2d at 1488.

court was entitled to weigh the evidence as a trier of fact. Upon reviewing the evidence presented to the district court in the light most favorable to Rosetta Stone as the nonmoving party, the Fourth Circuit concluded that the evidence was sufficient to establish a question of fact as to whether Google continued to knowingly supply its services to infringers. The court remanded the issue to the district court for further proceedings.

8

Domain Name Registration, Maintenance and Protection

Stephen Feingold
Kilpatrick Townsend & Stockton LLP
New York, NY
Howard S. Hogan
Gibson, Dunn & Crutcher LLP
Washington, D.C.

IV. The Anti-Cybersquatting Consumer Protection Act

A. Overview

[194][Add the following text at the beginning of footnote 194.] A trademark owner who has since abandoned its mark may also have standing to bring a claim under the ACPA for the redress of past injuries. *See* Fancaster, Inc. v. Comcast Corp., No. 08-2922, 2012 U.S. Dist. LEXIS 32287, at *17–19 (D.N.J. Mar. 9, 2012) (although it lacked standing to seek actual damages and injunctive relief, a cable company no longer using its mark could still pursue a cybersquatting claim to recover statutory damages for past violations).

[217][In footnote 217, correct the *In re Mohammad Gharbi* citation to read as follows.] 2011 Bankr. LEXIS 864, at *17–18 (W.D. Tex. Mar. 3, 2011).

[218][Add the following text at the end of footnote 218.] *See also* AIRFX. com v. AirFX, LLC, CV 11-01064, 2011 U.S. Dist. LEXIS 121772, at *6–7 (D. Ariz. Oct. 20, 2011) (identifying the elements of a reverse hijacking claim and noting that a UDRP decision to transfer the subject domain name, even though such transfer has not yet occurred, satisfies ACPA's requirement that the domain name be "suspended, disabled or transferred"). In *AIRFX.com*, the court acknowledged that while the Ninth Circuit had "not yet considered the issue," other appellate courts have held that a UDRP decision "triggers the right to sue." *Id.* (internal citation omitted).

[221][In footnote 221, correct the *Hawes* citation to read as follows.] 337 F.3d 377, 387, 67 USPQ2d 1276 (4th Cir. 2003).

[225][Add the following text at the end of footnote 225.] *See also* ISystems v. Spark Networks, Ltd., No. 10-10905, 2012 U.S. App. LEXIS 6197, at *7–8 (5th Cir. Mar. 21, 2012) (unpublished) (plaintiff sufficiently pled that defendant owners of "JDate," in obtaining plaintiff's "jdate.net" domain name through a National Arbitration Forum (NAF) proceeding, engaged in a "knowing and material misrepresentation" in violation of the ACPA by making a "material" change in blacking out portions of screen shots of plaintiff's Web site).

[Add the following text at the end of the section.]

In *Petroliam Nasional Berhad v. GoDaddy.com, Inc.*,[1] the U.S. District Court for the Northern District of California adjudicated the issue of domain name registrar liability on summary judgment, and held that Go Daddy's forwarding of domain names to a third-party Web site via an automated process did not constitute "use" under the ACPA.[2] The court explained: "Go Daddy simply provided the infrastructure to the registrant to route the disputed domains to the website of his choosing. Only the domain name registrant or the registrant's authorized licensee can 'use' a domain name for purposes of the ACPA."[3] The court also dismissed the plaintiff's claim of contributory cybersquatting on grounds that Go Daddy's domain name registration and routing services did not involve the type of "direct control and monitoring" necessary to support a claim of contributory infringement.[4] The court based this ruling on the additional grounds that no direct infringement by the registrant had occurred.[5] In theory, though, the *Petroliam* court's holding could be read to imply that

---

[1]No. C 09-5939, 2012 U.S. Dist. LEXIS 156, 101 USPQ2d 1507 (N.D. Cal. Jan. 3, 2012).

[2]*Id.* at *23, 101 USPQ2d at 1514.

[3]*Id.* at *24, 101 USPQ2d at 1514–15. The court, therefore, did not reach Go Daddy's alternative argument that it was protected under the ACPA's safe harbor provision for registrars. *Id.* at *15, 101 USPQ2d at 1512.

[4]*Id.* at *32, 101 USPQ2d at 1516. *See also* Chapter 7, Section XVI of the main volume and of the supplement (describing contributory trademark infringement claims).

[5]*Petroliam Nasional Berhad*, 2012 U.S. Dist. LEXIS 156, at *33, 101 USPQ2d at 1517.

a registrar could be found liable for contributory infringement if there is direct infringement and the registrar contributes to that infringement by engaging in activities that involve "direct control and monitoring."

D. Disputes Under the ACPA

[282][Add the following text at the end of footnote 282.] In subsequent proceedings in *HER, Inc.*, the court later awarded statutory damages in the amount of $20,000 for each of the subject domain names based on defendants' "willful, deliberate, bad faith intent to profit and their willful and malicious violations of the ACPA." HER, Inc. v. RE/MAX First Choice, LLC, No. C2-06-492, 2011 U.S. Dist. LEXIS 138132, at *8 (S.D. Ohio Dec. 1, 2011). *See also* Two Plus Two Publishing, LLC v. Boyd, No. 2:09-CV-02318, 2012 U.S. Dist. LEXIS 27545, at *14 (D. Nev. Mar. 1, 2012) (granting summary judgment for plaintiff on its ACPA claim and awarding statutory damages plus fees and costs).

[Add the following text at the end of the section.]

In determining whether a cybersquatting claim is barred by laches, courts consider the defendant's level of investment in its mark "'as the identity of the business in the minds of the public'" before suit is filed.[6] For example, in *AIRFX.com v. AirFX, LLC*, the U.S. District Court for the District of Arizona held that the defendant was not prejudiced by the trademark owner's delay in bringing suit because the defendant had not yet publicly announced its business and the subject domain name was still "parked" at the registrar's advertisement "splash page."[7]

VI. DOMAIN NAMES AS PROPERTY

[304a][Add new footnote 304a after "property," in the first line of the carry-over paragraph on page 508.] Foreign courts have also recognized that the prevailing judicial and academic view is that domain names should be considered a form of property. *See, e.g.*, Tucows.Com Co. v. Lojas Renner S.A. (2011), 106 O.R. 3d 561 (Can. Ont. C.A.) (surveying international judicial opinions and academic commentators and concluding that domain names are a form of "personal property" under the Canadian *Rules of Civil Procedure*).

[305][Add the following text at the end of footnote 305.] *But see In re* Forchion, 198 Cal. App. 4th 1284, 1308, 130 Cal. Rptr. 3d 690, 709 (2011) (noting, as dicta, that "[d]omain name registrants seemingly appear to

---

[6]AIRFX.com v. AirFX, LLC, No. CV 11-01064, 2012 U.S. Dist. LEXIS 43919, at *9 (D. Ariz. Mar. 29, 2012) (quoting Internet Specialties West, Inc. v. Milon-DiGiorgio Enters., Inc., 559 F. 3d 985, 992, 90 USPQ2d 1151, 1155 (9th Cir. 2009)).

[7]*Id.* at *10.

possess all three component rights [to be considered property under California law]. Upon closer analysis of the formation of domain names, however, it becomes apparent that a domain name is not property, but rather the product of a contract for services between the registrant and the registrar").

VII. COUNTRY CODE TOP-LEVEL DOMAINS

B. ccTLDs as Commercial Entities

[Add the following text at the end of the last paragraph on page 513.]

In October 2011, the registry for the Norwegian .no ccTLD blocked the registrant for the .co.no domain from going live due to concerns that the domain had been "intensively marketed as a way into the Norwegian domain market for foreign parties."[8] The dispute was scheduled to be heard before a Norwegian court in mid-2012.

C. ccTLDs as Property

[359][Add the following at the end of footnote 359.] Ironically, the Swiss government may have inadvertently demonstrated that ccTLDs are, as a practical matter, interchangeable with privately maintained domain name registries. When ICANN invited applications for private entities to maintain new Top Level Domain registries in 2012 (*see* Section VIII of this supplement), the Swiss government announced that it submitted an application for the ".SWISS" generic top level domain name in order "to safeguard the interests of Switzerland" because "the international recognition value of .SWISS is significantly higher than '.CH'—Switzerland's" ccTLD. Daniel Pruzin, *Swiss Government to Seek Control Over '.Swiss' gTLD*, 17 ELEC. COM. & LAW REP 1113 (June 14, 2012). As of the date of this writing, the Swiss government had "not yet decided" whether it would be directly responsible for the attribution of domain names under the .SWISS gTLD "or attribute it to a private sector entity, as is currently the case with the .CH ccTLD." *Id.*

VIII. NEW TOP-LEVEL DOMAINS

[365][Replace the URL in footnote 365 with the following.] http://archive.icann.org/en/tlds/tld-criteria-15aug00.htm (last visited June 1, 2012).

---

[8]NORID, Legal dispute about co.no, *available at* http://www.norid.no/nytt/co-tvist.en.html (last visited June 1, 2012).

[In the last paragraph of the section on page 515, delete the remainder of the paragraph starting with the fourth sentence (which begins "At the time of this writing, …") and add the following text at the end of the section.]

The period in which to register as a gTLD applicant for the first round of gTLD applications closed on May 30, 2012. ICANN reported that the number of registered applicants was 839, although each registrant was able to apply for up to fifty new gTLDs.[9] The window for completing applications was initially slated to close on April 12, 2012; however, on that date ICANN took the gTLD application system offline as a result of security concerns, as applicants who had previously deleted a file were able to see usernames and file names belonging to other applicants, though not the contents of the files.[10] On June 13, 2012, ICANN revealed the names of the companies that had applied for gTLD names in what it billed as the largest expansion in the history of the Internet's Domain Name System.[11] ICANN received 1,930 applications, with 911 from North America, 675 from Europe, 303 from the Asia-Pacific region, 24 from Latin America and the Caribbean, and 17 from Africa.[12] A quick review of the list shows that hundreds of companies and organizations applied to establish registries for their brand names, such as .AAA for the American Automobile Association and .BING for Microsoft's search engine brand. As expected, there were also multiple applicants for such generic terms as .AUTO, .CASINO, and .LLC. Some of the applicants were recognizable companies, while others, such as DotMusic Inc. and .Music LLC (which are competing with others for the .MUSIC registry), appear to have been incorporated for the express purpose of running one of these registries.

[Revise the Section VIII.A heading to read as follows.]

A.   What Is The Value of the New TLDs? [Revised Heading]

B.   Protecting Brand Owner Rights With Respect to New TLDs

[In the first sentence of the first paragraph of the section on page 516, delete the words "current draft."]

---

[9] ICANN, Program Statistics (2012), *available at* http://newgtlds.icann.org/en/program-status/statistics (last visited April 26, 2012).

[10] ICANN, Interview with ICANN Chief Security Officer Jeff Moss (2012), *available at* http://newgtlds.icann.org/en/announcements-and-media/video/cso-tas-19apr12-en (last visited April 26, 2012).

[11] *See* http://www.icann.org/en/news/announcements/announcement-13jun12-en.htm (last visited June 13, 2012). The full list is available at http://newgtlds.icann.org/en/program-status/application-results/strings-1200utc-13jun12-en (last visited June 13, 2012).

[12] *See* http://www.icann.org/en/news/announcements/announcement-13jun12-en.htm (last visited June 13, 2012).

[370][Replace the text of footnote 370 with the following.] ICANN, gTLD Applicant Guidebook at 7–10, *available at* http://newgtlds.icann.org/en/applicants/agb/guidebook-full-11jan12-en.pdf (last visited April 26, 2012).

[372][Replace the text of footnote 372 with the following.] *Id.* at 154.

C. Protecting Brand Owner Rights in Each TLD

[In the third sentence of the paragraph on page 517, replace "is currently considering" with "contemplates."]

[375][Replace the text of footnote 375 with the following.] *Id.* at 301.

[376][Replace the text of footnote 376 with the following.] *Id.* at 310.

[377][Replace the text of footnote 377 with the following.] *Id.* at 317.

D. Conclusion

[Add the following text at the end of the section.]

Although the high price tag associated with the application process appears to have, thus far, minimized the number of applicants who are obviously applying to obtain a registry in another company's brand name (analogous to cybersquatting), there are a number of instances in which multiple applicants may lay claim to the same name, or in which an applicant has applied for a registry that has both generic and trademark meaning. For example, Charleston Road Registry Inc., has applied for the .ANDROID registry.[13] The word "android" not only has a dictionary meaning, but is also the subject of numerous U.S. trademark registrations and is commonly associated with Google's popular mobile communications technology. The larger issue for trademark owners is the number of companies that applied to register generic terms as gTLDs, which then pose the risk of wreaking havoc if they are not diligent in preventing the registration of domain names associated with those gTLDs that are likely to cause trademark confusion (for example, if unauthorized parties are allowed to use the .CARS registry to register domain names like "Chevy.cars" or "Toyota.cars"). Only time will tell if the procedures that ICANN has established, and the federal courts, are up to the challenge.

---

[13] *See* http://newgtlds.icann.org/en/program-status/application-results/strings-1200utc-13jun12-en (last visited June 13, 2012).

9

Protection of Content in the Online Environment

Michael Ridgway Jones
Loeb & Loeb
New York, New York

Vesna N. Rafaty
Rafaty Law Group, PLLC
Richardson, Texas

Yakov Ginzburg
The Capital Group Companies, Inc.
Los Angeles, California

103

I. The Enforceability of Online Agreements

G. Clickwrap Agreements

[Add the following text at the end of the section.]

In a recent order granting AT&T Mobility's motion to compel arbitration, the United States District Court for the Northern District of California found that a wireless subscriber had accepted AT&T Mobility's terms of service by clicking a check box labeled "I have read and agree to the Service Agreement under the terms and conditions listed above" below a scrolling text box containing the terms of service.[1]

H. Browsewrap Cases

[44a] [Add the following new footnote, 44a, at the end of the last line of Section I.H on page 535.] A 2012 case illustrates the use of an old-fashioned paper notice to confirm what appear to have been, at best, confusingly presented online terms. In *Grosvenor v. Qwest Corp.*, No. 09-cv-02848, 2012 WL 602655, 2012 U.S. Dist. LEXIS 23472 (D. Colo. Feb. 23, 2012), a Colorado federal court applied the standard articulated in *Specht* to find that the plaintiff customer had unambiguously assented to terms of service that were made available to the customer via an online "I accept" button and subsequently confirmed by a written "welcome letter." *Id.* at *9, 2012 U.S. Dist. LEXIS 23472, at *24. Although the court noted that the "presentation of the terms is hardly a model of clarity," requiring the customer to click on two separate hyperlinks before being presented with the terms of use in a scrolling text box, the court nevertheless found that they were "sufficiently conspicuous," especially when confirmed by the follow-up welcome letter, which would be "sufficient to cure a reasonable user's confusion." *Id.* at *8, 2012 U.S. Dist. LEXIS 23472, at *24; *accord Vernon v. Qwest Commc'ns Int'l, Inc.*, No. 09-cv-01840, 2012 WL 768125, at *12, 2012 U.S. Dist. LEXIS 31076, at*42 (D. Colo. Mar. 8, 2012).

[Add the following text at the end of the section.]

A recent decision by a New York state court also illustrates the risk of "burying" terms of service under layers of Web pages. In *Jerez v. JD Closeouts, LLC*,[2] a New York customer sued a Florida seller seeking a refund of money paid via seller's e-commerce Web site.[3] The defendants argued that the case should have been brought in Florida based on the forum selection clause contained in the Web site's terms of sale.[4] The terms of

---

[1]Blau v. AT&T Mobility, No. C 11-00541, 2012 WL 566565, at *1–2, 2012 U.S. Dist. LEXIS 21458, at *4–5 (N.D. Cal. Feb. 21, 2012); *accord* Sherman v. AT&T Inc., No. 11 C 5857, 2012 WL 1021823, 2012 U.S. Dist. LEXIS 40394 (N.D. Ill. Mar. 26, 2012); Serrano v. Cablevision Sys. Corp., No. 09-CV-1056, 2012 WL 1040019, at *5, 2012 U.S. Dist. LEXIS 42152 (E.D.N.Y. Mar. 27, 2012); Kraft Real Estate Invs., LLC v. HomeAway.com, Inc., No. 4:08-CV-3788, 2012 WL 220271, 2012 U.S. Dist. LEXIS 8282 (D.S.C. Jan. 24, 2012) (affirming the enforceability of click-through online terms); *but see id.* at *10, 2012 U.S. Dist. LEXIS 8282, at *32–34–34 (refusing to enforce pure browsewrap terms where there was no evidence presented that plaintiff was actually aware of or had assented to terms posted via a hyperlink on Web site home page).
[2]No. CV-024727-11, 2012 WL 934390, 2012 N.Y. Misc. LEXIS 1224 (N.Y. Dist. Ct., Nassau Co., Mar. 20, 2012).
[3]*Id.* at *2, 2012 N.Y. Misc. LEXIS 1224, at *4.
[4]*Id.* at *1, 2012 N.Y. Misc. LEXIS 1224, at *2.

sale were available via a hyperlink on the Web site's "About Us" page.[5] The court, however, refused to enforce the terms and found that because the terms were "buried" and "submerged" on a Web page that "could only be found by clicking on an inconspicuous link on the company's 'About Us' page," the terms were not "reasonably communicated" to the user.[6] The court cautioned: "[T]his Court reiterates that forum selection clauses are *prima facie* valid when a party can show that the clause was incorporated into the parties' contract. However, e-commerce merchants cannot blithely assume that the inclusion of sale terms, listed somewhere on a hyper-linked page on its Web site, will be deemed part of any contract of sale."[7]

Similarly, in *Kwan v. Clearwire Corp.*,[8] a Washington federal court found that the plaintiffs were not bound by an arbitration clause contained in the defendant's terms of service because the plaintiffs were provided inadequate notice of, and did not unambiguously assent to, the terms.[9] The "placement" of the terms in *Kwan* is instructive. Here, Clearwire sent order confirmation emails to the plaintiffs which included a general link to Clearwire's home page at www.clearwire.com.[10] The home page, however, contained no reference to the terms of service and only displayed a hyperlink (located that the bottom of the page) to "legal."[11] A user clicking the "legal" hyperlink would then be taken to a second Web page which listed other hyperlinks alphabetically, including the terms of service, located on the bottom half of that page.[12] Only upon clicking the "terms of service" link would a user actually be able to review the terms, located on a third Web page.[13] Unsurprisingly, following the reasoning of *Specht*, the court found that "the breadcrumbs left by Clearwire to lead" the plaintiffs to its terms of service "did not constitute sufficient or reasonably conspicuous notice" of the terms of service.[14]

---

[5] *Id.* at *2, 2012 N.Y. Misc. LEXIS 1224, at *5.

[6] *Id.* at *6, 2012 N.Y. Misc. LEXIS 1224, at *15–16.

[7] *Id.* at *7, 2012 N.Y. Misc. LEXIS 1224, at *17; *see also* Mendelsohn v. BidCactus, LLC, No. 3:11-CV-1500, 2012 WL 1059702, at *8, 2012 U.S. Dist. LEXIS 42625, at *23 (D. Conn. Mar. 28, 2012) (finding that no express contract existed between plaintiff and defendant auction Web site provider because plaintiff was not required to affirmatively agree to Web site's terms of use in order to register for an account).

[8] No. C09-1392, 2012 WL 32380, 2011 U.S. Dist. LEXIS 150145 (W.D. Wash. Jan. 3, 2012).

[9] *Id.* at *9–10, 2011 U.S. Dist. LEXIS 150145, at *29–31.

[10] *Id.* at *2, 2011 U.S. Dist. LEXIS 150145, at *5.

[11] *Id.*, 2011 U.S. Dist. LEXIS 150145, at *5–6.

[12] *Id.*, 2011 U.S. Dist. LEXIS 150145, at *6.

[13] *Id.*, 2011 U.S. Dist. LEXIS 150145, at *6.

[14] *Id.* at *9, 2011 U.S. Dist. LEXIS 150145, at *27. A factual dispute remained as to whether one of the plaintiffs had actual or constructive notice of the terms of service even though she "specifically declined to press the 'I accept terms' button presented on Clearwire's webpage." *Id.* at *10, 2011 U.S. Dist. LEXIS 150145, at *32. *Accord* Liberty Syndicates at Lloyd's v. Walnut Advisory Corp., No. 09-1343, 2011 WL 5825777, at *5–6, 2011 U.S. Dist. LEXIS 132172, at *15–16 (D.N.J. Nov. 16, 2011) (finding that users had inadequate notice of a forum selection clause contained in a "terms of business agreement" available via a hyperlink in an e-mail footer).

[Add the following new section.]

1.   *Browsewrap/Clickwrap Hybrids [New Topic]*

As business practices have developed—and as users (and courts) have grown more accustomed to acknowledging the effect of online terms—certain methods of presentation that combine the characteristic features of clickwrap and browsewrap agreements have arisen. Instructive in this regard is the recent decision by a New York federal court in *Fteja v. Facebook, Inc.*[15] The district court held that the forum selection clause contained in Facebook's terms of service requiring all actions to be brought in California had been reasonably communicated to users. The court found that in registering to use Facebook, the plaintiff had been required to click a button marked "Sign Up" immediately above the following text: "By clicking Sign Up, you are indicating that you have read and agree to the Terms of Service."[16] The phrase "Terms of Service" was hyperlinked to the text of the terms.[17] The court discussed earlier cases such as *Register.com* and *Specht* and found that while *Specht* was not controlling, the case was similar in that "the terms and conditions were not displayed on the page where the user purportedly assented to the terms. Instead, those terms were visible only by clicking on a hyperlink."[18] Nevertheless, the *Fteja* agreement was not a traditional browsewrap agreement in that it required some actual manifestation of consent (i.e., clicking the "Sign Up" button) in order to bind the user to the terms. To this extent, the Facebook terms in *Fteja* resemble a clickwrap agreement.[19] But here, too, the court notes that the Facebook terms are not a pure clickwrap agreement either, because they do not require the user to actually scroll through or otherwise review the terms before manifesting assent.[20] The court summarized its conclusion as follows: "Facebook's Terms of Use are somewhat like a browsewrap agreement in that the terms are only visible via a hyperlink, but also somewhat like a clickwrap agreement in that the

---

[15]841 F. Supp. 2d 829, No. 11 Civ. 918, 2012 WL 183896, 2012 U.S. Dist. LEXIS 12991 (S.D.N.Y. Jan. 24, 2012).

[16]*Id.*, 2012 WL 183896, at *5, 2012 U.S. Dist. LEXIS 12991, at *12.

[17]*Id.*, 2012 U.S. Dist. LEXIS 12991, at *12.

[18]*Id.* at *6, 2012 U.S. Dist. LEXIS 12991, at *14–15. "The Terms of Use therefore appear to be a kind of so-called 'browsewrap' agreement, 'where website terms and conditions of use are posted on the website typically as a hyperlink at the bottom of the screen.'" *Id.*, 2012 U.S. Dist. LEXIS 12991, at *15 (quoting Hines v. Overstock.com, Inc., 668 F. Supp. 2d 362, 366 (E.D.N.Y. 2009)). "'[A] browse wrap license is part of the website and the user assents to the contract when the user visits the website.'" *Id.*, 2012 U.S. Dist. LEXIS 12991, at *15 (quoting Pollstar v. Gigmania Ltd., 170 F. Supp. 2d 974, 981 (E.D. Cal. 2000)). While noting that a number of courts have enforced browsewrap agreements, the court observed that many of these decisions involved business-to-business transactions, rather than business-to-consumer transactions as here (and as in *Specht*). *Id.*, 2012 U.S. Dist. LEXIS 12991, at *17 (citing Mark A. Lemley, *Terms of Use*, 91 MINN. L. REV. 459, 472 (2006)).

[19]*Id.* at *7, 2012 U.S. Dist. LEXIS 12991, at *19.

[20]*Id.* at *8, 2012 U.S. Dist. LEXIS 12991, at *21.

user must do something else—click 'Sign Up'—to assent to the hyper-linked terms. Yet, unlike some clickwrap agreements, the user can click to assent whether or not the user has been presented with the terms."[21]

Analogizing to the Supreme Court's well-known decision in *Carnival Cruise Lines, Inc. v. Shute*,[22] enforcing a forum selection clause printed in fine print on the back of a customer's ticket, the court in *Fteja* found that "clicking the hyperlinked phrase ['Terms of Service'] is the twenty-first century equivalent of turning over the cruise ticket" and held that Facebook's forum selection clause was valid and enforceable.[23]

I.   Modified Terms

[Add the following text after the carry-over paragraph on page 536.]

Similarly, in *Fraley v. Facebook, Inc.*,[24] the court rejected Facebook's motion to dismiss in part because it found there to be a disputed issue of fact as to whether the plaintiffs had validly consented to a provision in Facebook's Statement of Rights and Responsibilities that purported to allow Facebook to incorporate users' names, images and likenesses into "Sponsored Stories" advertisements to be used for Facebook's commercial gain.[25] The plaintiffs argued that at the time they joined Facebook, the Statement of Rights and Responsibilities said nothing about the "Sponsored Stories" feature, which indeed had been launched only subsequently and on an opt-out basis, meaning that users were automatically opted-in to the feature.[26] The Statement of Rights and Responsibilities was later revised to disclose this use of users' names, images and likenesses, but users were never asked to review this revised version, much less assent to it.[27] Moreover, the court refused to dismiss a separate allegation that Facebook had acted fraudulently by "knowingly and intentionally failing to seek and acquire members' informed consent regarding changes" to the Statement of Rights and Responsibilities.[28]

[At the beginning of the full paragraph on page 536, replace "If licensors appropriate notice ..." with "If licensors provide appropriate no-tice ...."]

---

[21] *Id.*, 2012 U.S. Dist. LEXIS 12991, at *23.

[22] 499 U.S. 585, 587 (1991).

[23] *Fteja*, 2012 WL 183896, at *9, 2012 U.S. Dist. LEXIS 12991, at *26–27. To support its decision, the *Fteja* court cited *Hubbert v. Dell Corp.*, 835 N.E.2d 113, 118, 121 (Ill. Ct. App. 2005), *Major v. McCallister*, 302 S.W.3d 227 (Mo. Ct. App. 2009), and *Snap-On Business Solutions, Inc. v. O'Neil & Assocs., Inc.*, 708 F. Supp. 2d 669 (N.D. Ohio 2010).

[24] 830 F. Supp. 2d 785 (N.D. Cal. 2011).

[25] *Id.* at 806.

[26] *Id.* at 792, 805, 814.

[27] *Id.* at 805

[28] *Id.* at 814.

[Revise the Section II, Section II.B, and Section II.C headings to read as follows.]

II. Trade Dress Protection of Web Sites

B. Trade Dress Protection of a Web Site

C. The Protectable "Look and Feel" of a Web Site

IV. Overview of Privacy Issues in Cloud Computing

C. Privacy Protections in the United States

[Add the following new sections.]

1. Framework for Protecting Privacy and Promoting Innovation in the Global Digital Economy [New Topic]

In February 2012, the White House issued *Consumer Data Privacy in a Networked World: A Framework for Protecting Privacy and Promoting Innovation in the Global Digital Economy* ("*Framework*").[29] The *Framework* aims to strengthen the existing consumer data privacy in the United States with "a clear statement of basic privacy principles that apply to the commercial world, and a sustained commitment of all stakeholders to address consumer data privacy issues as they arise from advances in technologies and business models."[30]

The *Framework* is concerned only with how private-sector entities handle personal data in online commercial settings, and consists of four key elements:

- A *Consumer Privacy Bill of Rights* setting forth individual rights and corresponding obligations of companies with respect to personal data. These consumer rights are based on U.S.-developed and globally recognized Fair Information Practice Principles (FIPPs), articulated in terms that apply to the dynamic environment of the Internet age;

---

[29]The full text of the Framework is available at http://www.whitehouse.gov/sites/default/files/privacy-final.pdf (Feb. 2012) (hereinafter *Framework*). *See also* Office of the Press Secretary, The White House, *We Can't Wait: Obama Administration Unveils Blueprint for a "Privacy Bill of Rights" to Protect Consumers Online* (Feb. 23, 2012), *available at* http://www.whitehouse.gov/the-press-office/2012/02/23/we-can-t-wait-obama-administration-unveils-blueprint-privacy-bill-rights.

[30]*Framework* at i.

- *Enforceable codes of conduct,* developed through *multi-stakeholder processes,* to form the basis for specifying what the Consumer Privacy Bill of Rights requires in particular business contexts;

- Federal Trade Commission (FTC) *enforcement* of consumers' data privacy rights through its authority to prohibit unfair or deceptive acts or practices; and

- Increasing *global interoperability* between the U.S. consumer data privacy framework and other countries' frameworks, through mutual recognition, the development of codes of conduct through multi-stakeholder processes, and enforcement cooperation can reduce barriers to the flow of information.[31]

Since the Consumer Privacy Bill of Rights is the centerpiece of the *Framework* and has the most direct and important implications to the privacy of the consumer data in the Cloud, it will be discussed in detail along with the administration's recommendations on implementing legislation.

2.   *Consumer Privacy Bill of Rights [New Topic]*

The Consumer Privacy Bill of Rights ("Bill of Rights") has important implications for privacy in the Cloud because of its broad and flexible definition of the personal data. The Bill of Rights "applies to commercial uses of personal data."[32] The term "personal data" refers to any data, including aggregations of data, of a specific individual. "Personal data may include data that is linked to a specific computer or other device."[33] Thus, Cloud service providers that store consumers' personal email messages, documents, photos and videos, will have to operate within the boundaries of the Bill of Rights.

The primary goal of The Consumer Bill of Rights (Bill of Rights) is to protect consumers' privacy expectations in online environment while providing companies (including Cloud services providers) with the certainty they need to continue to innovate. To achieve this goal, the Bill of Rights applies globally recognized Fair Information Practice Principles (FIPPs)[34] in two ways. First, it defines a set of consumer rights with respect to their personal data that is handled by the companies to which the

---

[31] *Id.* at 7 (emphasis in original). *See also id.* at 1.

[32] *Id.* at 10.

[33] *Id.*

[34] "Over the past quarter century, government agencies in the United States, Canada, and Europe have studied the manner in which entities collect and use personal information—their 'information practices'—and the safeguards required to assure those practices are fair and provide adequate privacy protection. The result has been a series of reports, guidelines, and model codes that represent widely-accepted principles concerning fair information practices. Common to all of these documents ... are five core principles of privacy protection: (1) Notice/Awareness; (2) Choice/Consent; (3) Access/Participation; (4) Integrity/Security; and (5) Enforcement/Redress." FTC, Fair Information Practice Principles, *available at* http://www.ftc.gov/reports/privacy3/fairinfo.shtm (footnotes omitted).

consumers have entrusted their data. Second, the Bill of Rights outlines various contexts under which the consumers' right may be exercised.[35]

The Bill of Rights advances its objectives by holding that consumers have a right to: (a) Individual Control; (b) Transparency; (c) Respect for Context; (d) Security; (e) Access and Accuracy; (f) Focused Collection; and (g) Accountability.[36]

a.   Individual Control [New Topic]

The Individual Control principle provides that "[c]consumers have a right to exercise control over what personal data companies collect from them and how they use it."[37] The Bill of Rights envisions that both companies and consumers will have to cooperate to ensure this right. The Bill of Rights (i) creates obligations for companies that handle their customers' private data; and (ii) defines the responsibilities of the consumers that share their data.

i.   Companies' Obligations to the Consumers [New Topic]

Companies should provide consumers with easy and accessible mechanisms to control the collection, use, or disclosure of their personal data by the service providers. In addition, these tools must be provided at the times that will enable the consumers to make the meaningful choices about their personal data.[38]

The Bill of Rights recognizes that ensuring this right where there is no direct interaction between the company and the consumers is a challenge. In this case, the Bill suggests that such providers (e.g., data brokers and Cloud services providers) may use other principles from the Bill to ensure customers' individual control over their data. For example, the companies may provide clear and public explanations of the roles they play in commercial uses of personal data (a Transparency principle). Additionally, the companies may provide the consumers with appropriate data usage controls once the information is collected under Access and Accuracy and Accountability principles.[39]

It is still unclear how this principle can be effectively implemented in the dynamic world of sub-contracting by Cloud service providers. For example, provisioning scalable data services to the consumers may require Cloud service providers to frequently add or change their sub-contractors. As a result, keeping their customers abreast with the changes having impact on their data privacy may introduce a significant burden on Cloud

---

[35] *Framework* at 9. "Key elements of context include the goals or purposes that consumers can expect to achieve by using a company's products or services, the services that the companies actually provide, the personal data exchanges that are necessary to provide these services, and whether a company's customers include children and adolescents. Context should shape the balance and relative emphasis of particular principles in the Consumer Privacy Bill of Rights." *Id.* at 9–10.

[36] *Id.* at 1, 10.

[37] *Id.* at 11.

[38] *Id.*

[39] *Id.* at 13.

service providers. Such burden may result in increased operating costs and additional overhead of administering the appropriate notices to the appropriate parties.

ii.   Consumers' Responsibility [New Topic]

The Bill of Rights contemplates that consumers have a responsibility in the initial act of sharing their information. Using the tools provided by the companies, the consumers have a responsibility to of making an educated and intelligent choice about sharing their personal data with others. This responsibility also includes the right to withdraw consent to use personal data that company controls. Thus, companies must provide the users with meaningful ways to withdraw their consent.[40]

b.   Transparency [New Topic]

The Transparency principle mandates that "[c]onsumers have a right to easily understandable and accessible information about [service providers'] privacy practices."[41] Securing this right may be a serious challenge for Cloud service provider sub-contractors that do not directly interact with the customers. While the Bill of Rights suggests that such providers may discharge this responsibility by posting relevant explanations on their Web sites, the practical effect of such disclosure could be minimal. First, the direct Cloud service provider may not be willing to disclose information about its sub-contractors. Second, even if the consumers know about all their Cloud service provider's sub-contractors, they would have to spend a considerable amount of time perusing and understanding various privacy disclosures.

c.   Respect for Context [New Topic]

The principle holds that "[c]onsumers have a right to expect that companies will collect, use, and disclose personal data in ways that are consistent with the context in which consumers provide the data."[42] However, ensuring proper boundaries of the context in the Cloud may not be as straight-forward as it may seem from a first glance.

For example, Google Docs, which invites the user to "create and share your work online," allows the user to create or upload documents containing different types of data onto the Google server. Oftentimes, there is no specific or stated purpose for such sharing except for the convenience of accessibility of the documents from any computer or mobile device. As such, it is unclear whether Google could violate the principle of respecting the context by automatically scanning the documents to provide most relevant advertising messages to the consumers.

---

[40] *Id.*

[41] *Id.* at 14.

[42] *Id.* at 15.

d.   Security [New Topic]

Under this principle, "[c]onsumers have a right to secure and responsible handling of personal data. Companies should assess the privacy and security risks associated with their personal data practices and maintain reasonable safeguards to control risks such as loss; unauthorized access, use, destruction, or modification; and improper disclosure."[43] The principle gives companies the discretion to choose the most appropriate technology to manage personal data, "subject to their obligations under any applicable data security statutes, including their duties to notify consumers and law enforcement agencies if the security of data about them is breached, and their commitments to adopt reasonable security practices."[44]

e.   Access and Accuracy [New Topic]

The principle holds that "[c]onsumers have a right to access and correct personal data in usable formats, in a manner that is appropriate to the sensitivity of the data and the risk of adverse consequences to consumers if the data is inaccurate."[45]

f.   Focused Collection [New Topic]

This principle holds that "[c]onsumers have a right to reasonable limits on the personal data that companies collect and retain. Companies should collect only as much personal data as they need to accomplish purposes specified under the Respect for Context principle. Companies should securely dispose of or de-identify personal data once they no longer need it, unless they are under a legal obligation to do otherwise."[46]

g.   Accountability [New Topic]

Under this principle, "[c]onsumers have a right to have personal data handled by companies with appropriate measures in place to assure they adhere to the Consumer Privacy Bill of Rights."[47] Under the Bill of Rights, such companies must train their employees to handle the personal data, regularly evaluate their performance, and conduct full audits where appropriate. In addition, companies that disclose personal data to the third parties such as Cloud service sub-contractors must contractually ensure the sub-contracting parties adhere to the Bill of Rights principles, unless the applicable laws demand otherwise.[48]

---

[43] *Id.* at 19.
[44] *Id.*
[45] *Id.*
[46] *Id.* at 20–21.
[47] *Id.* at 21.
[48] *Id.*

3.   *Enacting Consumer Privacy Legislation [New Topic]*

The *Framework* contemplates a flexible legislature guaranteeing consumers a set of basic set of privacy rights, and allowing companies to implement the Consumer Privacy Bill of Rights in ways that fit the context in which they do business.[49]

To centralize the enforcement of privacy laws, the Obama administration recommends that Congress grant the FTC the authority to enforce each element of the statutory Consumer Privacy Bill of Rights.[50] The administration also recommends that the FTC be given "the authority to grant a 'safe harbor'—that is, forbearance from enforcement of the statutory Consumer Privacy Bill of Rights—to companies that follow a code of conduct that the FTC has reviewed and approved. Companies that decline to adopt a code of conduct, or choose not to seek the FTC review of a code that they do adopt, would simply be subject to the general obligations of the legislatively adopted Consumer Privacy Bill of Rights."[51]

The administration also sees an advantage in balancing federal and state roles in consumer data privacy protection. An enacted Bill of Rights should provide a "national standard for protecting consumer data privacy where existing Federal data privacy statutes do not apply. Nationally uniform consumer data privacy rules are necessary to create certainty for companies and consistent protections for consumers."[52] While state laws would be preempted if in conflict with the provisions of a Bill of Rights, the states still would maintain policymaking and enforcement roles in the multi-stakeholder process.[53]

Additionally, legislation should "preserve existing sector-specific Federal laws that effectively protect personal data, minimize the duplication of legal requirements, and provide consumers with a clear sense of what protections they have and who enforces them."[54]

Finally, the *Framework* recommends the establishment of a national standard for security breach notification which would replace a patchwork of state laws regulating security breach notifications.[55]

E.   Stored Communications Act

[Add the following new section.]

---

[49] *Id.* at 35.

[50] *Id.* at 36.

[51] *Id.* at 37.

[52] *Id.*

[53] *Id.*

[54] *Id.* at 38.

[55] *Id.* at 39. "Currently, 47 States, the District of Columbia, and several U.S. Territories, have [Security Breach Notification] laws." *Id. See also the list of the States that have enacted Security Breach Notification laws at: http://www.ncsl.org/issues-research/telecom/ security-breach-notification-laws.aspx.*

1.   Electronic Communications Privacy Act Amendments Act of 2011 [New Topic]

On May 17, 2011, Senator Patrick Leahy introduced the Electronic Communications Privacy Act Amendments Act of 2011 "[t]o improve the provisions relating to the privacy of electronic communications."[56] While the Act would change numerous provisions of the Electronic Communications Privacy Act of 1986, Section 3 of the Act is the most relevant to privacy in the Cloud. Section 3 of the bill eliminates the so-called "180-day rule" and strengthens protection of the personal content stored in the Cloud against warrantless government search. If the bill were to be enacted, the government will be required to obtain a warrant for personal data searches regardless of the data's online age.[57]

I.   European Union Privacy Regime

[Add the following new sections.]

1.   Proposed EU General Data Protection Regulation [New Topic]

On January 25, 2012, the European Commission published its proposed EU General Data Protection Regulation (Proposed Regulation).[58] If enacted, the Proposed Regulation will replace the existing EU Data Protective Directive (Directive).[59] The Proposed Regulation would replace all national data protection laws of EU Member States once it becomes a law—unlike the Directive that had to be implemented individually by the EU members features of the Proposed Regulation are: (a) Consent; (b) Definition of Personal Data; (c) Accountability; (d) Right to be Forgotten; and (e) Data Security and Notifications.[60]

a.   Consent [New Topic]

The Proposed Regulation requires that consumers (data subjects) give an explicit consent to the data controllers to process personal data.

---

[56]S. 1011, 112th Cong. (2011) (Synopsis). The full text of the bill is available at http://www.gpo.gov/fdsys/pkg/BILLS-112s1011is/pdf/BILLS-112s1011is.pdf.

[57]According to govtrack.us, a Federal legislative tracking online service, as of May 2012, the chances that this bill will be enacted is only 3%. *See* http://www.govtrack.us/congress/bills/112/s1011.

[58]Proposal for a Regulation of the European Parliament and of the Council on the protection of individuals with regard to the processing of personal data and on the free movement of such data (General Data Protection Regulation), Eur. Par. Doc. (COM (2012) 11 final), *available at* http://ec.europa.eu/justice/data-protection/document/review2012/com_2012_11_en.pdf.

[59]See O.J. (L281)Directive 95/46/EC on the protection of individuals with regard to the processing of personal data and on the free movement of such data, O.J. (L281) (23.11.95). See also the complementary Council Framework Decision 2008/977/JHA of 27 November 2008 on the protection of personal data processed in the framework of police and judicial cooperation in criminal matters, O.J. (L 350) (30.12.2008).

[60]*See id.* at 15–19.

In addition, it places burden on the data controller to prove that the data subject has given a valid consent.[61] Finally, the Proposed Regulation provides that "consent shall not provide a legal basis for the processing where there is a significant imbalance between the position of the data subject and the data controller."[62] Cloud service providers have the ability to transfer data between multiple jurisdictions without consumers' knowledge. If this arrangement is deemed a "significant imbalance," this requirement may increase the burden of securing and proving valid consent to process data for Cloud service providers.

b.   Personal Data [New Topic]

The Proposed Regulation defines data subject as "'an identified natural person or a natural person who can be identified, directly or indirectly, by means reasonably likely to be used by the controller or by any other natural or legal person.'"[63] Such a broad definition of personal data "suggest that, even if the controller has undertaken all reasonable steps to de-identify the data processed, this data may still be considered to be personal data if anyone, anywhere, has the means to identify the individual, from a set of data previously and legitimately processed."[64]

c.   Accountability [New Topic]

The Proposed Regulation requires data controllers to implement appropriate measures to ensure that the processing of the personal data complies with the Proposed Regulation. Data controllers are also required to have ability to demonstrate that they are in compliance with the Proposed Regulation.[65]

d.   Right to be Forgotten [New Topic]

"The Proposed Regulation introduces a new 'right to be forgotten' which requires data controller to erase all personal data upon request from the data subject, and to take steps to erase all links to that data where the controller has made the data public."[66]

This requirement places an additional burden on Cloud service providers to ensure that the data is destroyed on all possible sub-contractors' servers. Policing such erasure may impossible to achieve without auditing the sub-contractors. Another complication may arise with the documents that consumers share with others using Cloud services, as in the use of Google Docs. If the document is now jointly owned, it is unclear whether providers will have to obtain the consent to erase the file from all involved parties.

---

[61] *See id.* at 15.

[62] *Id.* at 16 (quoting Art. 7(4) of the Proposed Regulation).

[63] *Id.* (quoting Art. 4(1) of the Proposed Regulation).

[64] *Id.*

[65] *Id.* at 16–17 (citing Arts. 35 and 36 of the Proposed Regulation).

[66] *Id.* at 17 (citing Art. 17(1) of the Proposed Regulation).

The Proposed Regulation provides a number of exemptions to the "right to be forgotten." If the data controllers determine that the data is necessary for historical, statistical, and scientific research purposes, they can retain the data.[67]

e.   Data Security and Notifications [New Topic]

"The Proposed Regulation requires data controllers to notify the relevant Data Protection Authorities of any personal data security breaches involving personal data, without undue delay and, where feasible, not later than 24 hours after having become aware of it."[68] The Proposed regulation also requires that individuals be notified of a security breach.[69]

J.   Privacy Regulations Around the World

[Add the following new section.]

1.   APEC Cross-Border Privacy Rules [New Topic]

In November 2011, the ministers of the Asia-Pacific Economic Cooperation forum (APEC)[70] endorsed the Cross-Border Privacy Rules (CBPRs) to both enhance data privacy practices and promote multi-country information flow and privacy regime interoperability.[71]

CBPRs are not privacy laws in themselves. Instead, they are rules developed by businesses that set out their practices in relation to any personal information they may collect from their customers. One of the key Privacy Principles underlying the CBPR system is Accountability.[72] A business will be accountable for the promises it makes to its customers about

---

[67] Id. (citing Art. 17(3)(c) of the Proposed Regulation).

[68] Id. 18 (citing Art. 31 of the Proposed Regulation). Long and Walch foresee logistical challenges and technical difficulties in carrying out this requirement. Id.

[69] Id. (citing Art. 32 of the Proposed Regulation). Again, Long and Walch recognize a potential problem with the requirement: "An efficient response to the breach would require that the data subject should not remain unaware of the breach whilst the Data Protection Authority has already been notified. In fact, earlier notification could allow the data subject to take urgent necessary steps to reduce the detrimental consequences of the breach …." Id.

[70] "Asia-Pacific Economic Cooperation, or APEC, is the premier forum for facilitating economic growth, cooperation, trade and investment in the Asia-Pacific region. APEC is the only inter governmental grouping in the world operating on the basis of non-binding commitments, open dialogue and equal respect for the views of all participants. Unlike the WTO or other multilateral trade bodies, APEC has no treaty obligations required of its participants. Decisions made within APEC are reached by consensus and commitments are undertaken on a voluntary basis." APEC, About APEC, available at http://www.apec.org/About-Us/About-APEC.aspx. The United States is a member-state of the APEC.

[71] See APEC, Statement, 2011 APEC Ministerial Meeting, available at http://www.apec.org/Meeting-Papers/Ministerial-Statements/Annual/2011/2011_amm.aspx.

[72] See generally APEC, APEC Cross-Border Privacy Enforcement Arrangement (2011), available at http://aimp.apec.org/Documents/2011/ECSG/DPS2/11_ecsg_dps2_010.pdf.

the way in which it will deal with their personal information. Accountability requires that there must be effective guidance for both business and consumers and effective enforcement of obligations throughout APEC economies.[73]

The APEC Privacy Framework (2004)[74] provides a method where an organization can be certified by an accountability agent.[75] "The accountability agent will compare the organization's cross-border privacy rules against a baseline and by being certified, the organization commits to following those rules. If it does not, it can be found in violation of a nation's privacy regime."[76]

---

[73] *Id.*

[74] *See* APEC Privacy Framework (2004), *available at* http://www.nacpec.org/docs/APEC_Privacy_Framework.pdf.

[75] "Accountability Agents are responsible for receiving an Applicant's intake documentation, verifying an Applicant's compliance with the requirements of the CBPR System and, where appropriate, assisting the Applicant in modifying its policies and practices to meet the requirements of the CBPR System." *See* APEC, APEC Cross-Border Privacy Rules System Program Requirements, *available at* http://www.apec.org/Groups/Committee-on-Trade-and-Investment/~/media/Files/Groups/ECSG/CBPR/CBPR-ProgramRequirements.ashx.

[76] Thomas Shaw, *2012 (1Q) Information Law Updates—Cases, Statutes and Standards,* ABA, Information Security & Privacy News, at 23, *available at* http://www.americanbar.org/content/dam/aba/administrative/science_technology/2012_isc_spring_v3i2.authcheckdam.pdf.

10

Patents and the Internet*

David Collado
Innovation Interactive
New York, New York

Li Dai
Ishimaru & Associates, LLP
San Jose, California

Stephanie Idio
Florida Coastal School of Law
Jacksonville, Florida

Rick Sanchez
Texas Wesleyan School of Law
Fort Worth, Texas

---

*The assistance of lawyer and editor David Reynaud, of Charlottesville, Virginia, is gratefully acknowledged.

I. PATENT REFORM AS IT APPLIES TO NON-PRACTICING ENTITY PATENT LITIGATION

A. Changes in Remedies and Damages

3. Changes in Methods for Calculating Damages

[Add the following text at the end of the section.]

Often times, previous license agreements involving an asserted patent are relevant to calculation of damages. Rule 408 of the Federal Rules of Evidence generally bars the admissibility of offers of settlement and settlement negotiations.[1] However, in patent cases, previous settlement offers and license agreements can be admissible if certain criteria are met. Below are situations in which intellectual property license agreements and offers of settlement can be admissible despite Rule 408 restrictions.

In *In re MSTG, Inc.*[2] the Federal Circuit ruled on whether a "settlement privilege" that protects negotiations leading to settlement agreements exists outside of mediation. The Federal Circuit held that negotiations leading to settlement and license agreements are discoverable. However, the admissibility of the agreements is protected by Federal Rules of Evidence 408 in certain circumstances.[3] The *MSTG* court explained that despite the circuit law split, this issue "has a significant bearing on the substantive issue of patent damages" and therefore the Federal Circuit can "apply [its] own law in determining whether a privilege or other discovery limitations protect disclosure of information related to reasonable royalties."[4] Because there is no codified statute discussing the settlement privilege, the issue was whether the Federal Circuit would create one for the discoverability of settlement negotiations (not for the settlements themselves) using the power of Federal Rules of Evidence 501 which allows the fashioning of new privileges based on common law.[5] The Federal Circuit decided not to create a new settlement privilege because: (1) there is no state consensus as to the existence of this privilege[6]; (2) Congress adopted Rule 408 addressing the admissibility of these negotiations and did not explicitly "take the additional step" to adopt a privilege about them while doing so[7]; (3) such a privilege was not included in the list of possible privileges enumerated by the Advisory Committee of the Judicial Confer-

---

[1] FED. R. EVID. 408.

[2] 675 F.3d 1337, 102 USPQ2d 1321 (Fed. Cir. 2012).

[3] *Id.* at 1346, 102 USPQ2d at 1327. Such circumstances are discussed below in this section.

[4] *Id.* at 1341–42, 102 USPQ2d at 1323–24.

[5] *Id.* at 1342–43, 102 USPQ2d at 1325.

[6] *Id.* at 1343, 102 USPQ2d at 1325 ("'the policy decisions of the States bear on the question whether federal courts should recognize a new privilege or amend the coverage of an existing one'") (quoting Jaffee v. Redmond, 518 U.S. 1, 12–13, (1996)).

[7] *Id.* at 1344, 102 USPQ2d at 1326.

ence for the Federal Rules of Evidence[8]; (4) the "need for confidence and trust alone" that promotes open dialogue in settlement discussions is "an insufficient reason to create a new privilege" and "disputes are routinely settled without the benefit of a settlement privilege"[9]; (5) any adopted privilege would have numerous exceptions and "'a[n] uncertain privilege … is little better than no privilege at all'"[10]; and (6) "there are other effective methods to limit the scope of discovery" to protect the sanctity of settlement discussions, such as protective orders under Federal Rules of Civil Procedure 26.[11] The court went on to note that other courts have required a party seeking discovery of confidential communications to make a "heightened showing" demonstrating "special need" and "unfairness."[12] (Again, this related to the discoverability of the negotiations, not their admissibility, which "[had] not yet [been] decided."[13]) "Because the issue is not before us, we reserve for another day the issue of what limits can appropriately be placed on discovery of settlement negotiations. But the existence of such authority, whatever its scope, strongly argues against the need for recognition of a privilege. In other words, the public policy goals argued to support a privilege can more appropriately be achieved by limiting the scope of discovery."[14]

However, the Federal Circuit does recognize that "all states have apparently enacted a statutory mediation privilege" regarding negotiations and communications.[15] In operation, parties could continue to argue that communications and drafts exchanged in the context of mediation are privileged, and could also argue that drafts and communications that continue to be exchanged after the mediation is over are still protected by the mediation privilege.

Outside of mediations however, it seems likely, given the factors above, that plaintiffs can still ask the court to protect these negotiation communications in a protective order or ask for some other form of protection from their discovery such as requiring that a requesting party make a "heightened showing" of its need for the communications. Defendants are not likely to agree, of course, but maybe there is some way to compromise. Otherwise, competing proposed protective orders can be submitted to the court. *In re MSTG* makes clear that a blanket "settlement privilege" for these communications—which are increasingly important in a patent damages and the reasonable royalty context—does not exist.

In 2010, the Federal Circuit decided *ResQNet.com v. Lansa, Inc.*,[16] which, among other issues, addressed the admissibility of several license agreements in the context of patent infringement litigation.

---

[8] *Id.* at 1345, 102 USPQ2d at 1326.

[9] *Id.*, 102 USPQ2d at 1326–27.

[10] *Id.* at 1345–46, 102 USPQ2d at 1327 (quoting *Jaffee*, 518 U.S. at 18).

[11] *Id.* at 1346, 102 USPQ2d at 1327.

[12] *Id.* at 1347, 102 USPQ2d at 1328.

[13] *Id.* at 1347 n.4, 102 USPQ2d at 1328 n.4.

[14] *Id.* at 1347, 102 USPQ2d at 1329.

[15] *Id.* at 1343, 102 USPQ2d at 1325 (citing Jay M. Zitter, Annotation, *Construction and Application of State Mediation Privilege*, 32 A.L.R. 6th 285, §2 (2008)).

[16] ResQNet.com v. Lansa, Inc., 594 F.3d 860, 93 USPQ2d 1553 (Fed. Cir. 2010).

ResQNet involved a suit over screen recognition and terminal emulation processes between a mainframe and PC. The plaintiff had received an infringement finding of one of ResQNet.com's patents (the '075 patent) and was awarded $506,305 in damages by the district court based largely on a 12.5 percent royalty rate adopted by the court. The royalty rate had been determined by plaintiff's expert who took into account several previous license agreements, some of which had no relation to the patent in suit.[17] In this case, the plaintiff's expert included license agreements that not only considered the technology covered by the patent-in-suit, but also relied on "re-bundling" licenses that sold more than just the patented technology and software.[18]

The Federal Circuit ultimately found that the inclusion of these licenses was not a relevant piece of evidence to submit to the jury and allow them to consider when assigning damages for the infringement. Instead, the court noted that on remand, the trial court "should not rely on unrelated licenses to increase the reasonable royalty rate above rates more clearly linked to the economic demand for the claimed technology."[19] If licenses are to be used as evidence to help determine a proper damage model, the plaintiff must link licenses to the infringed patent at issue.[20]

Often cited by *ResQNet*, and of particular importance to the subject was the 2009 *Lucent Technologies, Inc. v. Gateway, Inc.*[21] opinion by the Federal Circuit. In *Lucent*, the plaintiffs claimed patent infringement by Microsoft in its Outlook email and calendaring technology. At the trial court level, a jury awarded the plaintiffs lump-sum payment of roughly $358 million in damages.

The Federal Circuit reversed the damages based, among other things, that Lucent applied some "radically different" licenses to the proposed hypothetical negotiation model that was applied at trial.[22] The court noted that the evidence Lucent relied upon did not mesh with the scenario presented by the damages expert when explaining to the jury the damage model of applying a damages calculation based on a hypothetical negotiation between the two parties. The court also expressed concern that the subject matter of some of the other agreements could not be linked to the patent-at-issue and therefore should not have been considered either.[23]

One final precedent to consider is the order in *DataTreasury v. Wells Fargo*.[24] In this instance, the court excluded lump sum settlements because the plaintiff's damage model relied on a running royalty and not on a lump sum agreement. While on its face the order looks to ban lump-sum settlement agreements, the court noted that this was still a probative val-

[17] *Id.* at 868, 870, 93 USPQ2d at 1559, 1560.
[18] *Id.* at 870, 93 USPQ2d at 1561.
[19] *Id.* at 872–73, 93 USPQ2d at 1562.
[20] *Id.* at 871, 873, 93 USPQ2d at 1561, 1562.
[21] 580 F.3d 1301, 92 USPQ2d 1555 (Fed. Cir. 2009).
[22] *Id.* at 1327–28, 92 USPQ2d at 1574.
[23] *Id.* at 1328, 92 USPQ2d at 1574.
[24] DataTreasury Corp. v. Wells Fargo & Co., Order, C.A. No. 2:06-CV-72, Dkt. No. 2392 at 31 (Oct. 5, 2010) & Order, Dkt. No. 2052 (Mar. 16, 2010) (E.D. Tex.).

ue standard and license agreements that are not substantially outweighed by the danger of unfair prejudice are admissible. Thus, like the Federal Circuit precedent, the inquiry is one of probative value of the license agreement evidence and how closely comparable the license agreement is to the plaintiff's damage model.

In summary, the Federal Circuit standard seems to allow for license agreements to be relied upon by experts and presented at trial; however, the court will likely stifle such use if the license agreements do not involve the patent at suit or incorporate other patents or technology into one license agreement. If a license agreement covers the same ground and the same patent as the one that is the subject of the litigation, Federal Circuit law indicates that the license agreement can indeed be used for computation of damages.

5. Willful Infringement Standard

[Add the following text at the end of the section.]

Typically, evidence that was considered as part of the determination of whether an alleged infringer's acts were objectively reckless was whether or not an alleged infringer received advice of counsel as to whether it infringed the asserted patent. However, the Leahy-Smith America Invents Act ("AIA"),[25] enacted on September 16, 2011, eliminates use of evidence of a defendant's failure to acquire advice of counsel as proof of willful infringement. Section 17(a) of the AIA amends Chapter 29 by adding at its end, the following:

§298. Advice of counsel

The failure of an infringer to obtain the advice of counsel with respect to any allegedly infringed patent, or the failure of the infringer to present such advice to the court or jury, may not be used to prove that the accused infringer willfully infringed the patent or that the infringer intended to induce infringement of the patent.[26]

Section 35 of the AIA states that:

Except as otherwise provided in this Act, the provisions of this Act shall take effect upon the expiration of the 1-year period beginning on the date of the enactment of this Act and shall apply to any patent issued on or after that effective date.[27]

Therefore, Section 17 of the AIA (codified at 35 U.S.C. §298) is controlled by Section 35 and becomes effective September 16, 2012. Section 298 helps protect defendants in a patent action from liability for enhanced damages for willful infringement based on whether or not a patent opinion was obtained.

---

[25] 112 P.L. 29, 125 Stat. 284 (Sept. 16, 2011).
[26] Id. §17(a) (codified at 35 U.S.C. §298) (effective Sept. 16, 2012).
[27] Id. §35. See 35 U.S.C. §1 note.

[Add the following new section.]

6.   *Marking and Notice [New Topic]*

35 U.S.C. §287(a) provides:

> Patentees, and persons making, offering for sale, or selling within the United States any patented article for or under them, or importing any patented article into the United States, may give notice to the public that the same is patented, either by fixing thereon the word "patent" or the abbreviation "pat.", together with the number of the patent, or by fixing thereon the word "patent" or the abbreviation "pat." together with an address of a posting on the Internet, accessible to the public without charge for accessing the address, that associates the patented article with the number of the patent, or when, from the character of the article, this cannot be done, by fixing to it, or to the package wherein one or more of them is contained, a label containing a like notice. In the event of failure so to mark, no damages shall be recovered by the patentee in any action for infringement, except on proof that the infringer was notified of the infringement and continued to infringe thereafter, in which event damages may be recovered only for infringement occurring after such notice. Filing of an action for infringement shall constitute such notice.[28]

"[T]he plain language of [35 U.S.C. §287(a)] does not provide any time limit by which marking must begin," but recovery of damages is allowed from the point of full compliance with the marking statute.[29] The statute therefore "furthers the policy of encouraging marking to provide notice to the public, even if initial marking after issuance of the patent is delayed."[30] Once marking has begun in compliance with the statute, "*in rem* notice is provided and there is no reason to further limit damages on this account."[31]

The Federal Circuit cautions, however, that "once marking has begun, it must be substantially consistent and continuous in order for the party to avail itself of the constructive notice provisions of the statute."[32]

In *SRI International, Inc. v. Advanced Technology Laboratories, Inc.*,[33] SRI's patent counsel sent a notice letter to a potential infringer's president identifying two models and stating that those models might infringe one or more claims of the '750 patent. The letter went on to offer a nonexclusive license, and included a copy of the patent at issue and a reexamination certificate. The defendant argued that this letter did not constitute adequate notice of infringement "and that the accrual of damages should be limited to the date suit was filed."[34]

---

[28] 35 U.S.C. §287(a).
[29] American Med. Sys., Inc. v. Medical Eng'g Corp., 6 F.3d 1523, 1537, 28 USPQ2d 1321, 1331 (Fed. Cir. 1993). *See* 35 U.S.C. §287, Limitation on damages and other remedies; marking and notice.
[30] *American Med. Sys.*, 6 F.3d at 1537, 28 USPQ2d at 1332.
[31] *Id.*, 28 USPQ2d at 1332.
[32] *Id.*, 28 USPQ2d at 1332.
[33] 127 F.3d 1462, 44 USPQ2d 1422 (Fed. Cir. 1997).
[34] *Id.* at 1469, 44 USPQ2d at 1427–28.

The Federal District Court held that "[a]bsent marking, damages may be recovered only after actual notice is given."[35] "The criteria for actual notice under §287(a) are not coextensive with the criteria for filing a declaratory judgment action."[36] Section 287(a) requires actual notice to the accused "to assure that the recipient knew of the adverse patent during the period in which liability accrues, when constructive notice by marking is absent."[37] "Actual notice may be achieved without creating a case of actual controversy in terms of 28 U.S.C. Section 2201."[38] "It is not controlling whether the patentee threatens suit, demands cessation of infringement, or offers a license under the patent."[39] "[A]s long as the communication from the patentee provides sufficient specificity regarding its belief that the recipient may be an infringer, the statutory requirement of actual notice is met. Thus, the requirement of 'a specific charge of infringement' set forth in *Amsted* does not mean the patentee must make an 'unqualified charge of infringement.'"[40]

B. Changes in Patent Validity

[Add the following new section.]

4. *Patentable Subject Matter [New Topic]*

35 U.S.C. §101 defines the scope of inventions that are patentable:

> Whoever invents or discovers any new and useful process, machine, manufacture, or composition of matter, or any new and useful improvement thereof, may obtain a patent therefor, subject to the conditions and requirements of this title.[41]

The Supreme Court has held that "Congress intended statutory subject matter to 'include anything under the sun that is made by man.'"[42] "While a scientific truth, or the mathematical expression of it, is not patentable invention, a novel and useful structure created with the aid of knowledge of scientific truth may be."[43] "An idea of itself is not patentable."[44]

---

[35] *Id.*, 44 USPQ2d at 1428 (Fed. Cir. 1997).

[36] *Id.* at 1470, 44 USPQ2d at 1428.

[37] *Id.*, 44 USPQ2d at 1428. *See* Minks v. Polaris Indus., Inc., 546 F.3d 1364, 1376, 89 USPQ2d 1102, 1111 (Fed. Cir. 2008) (quoting *SRI*).

[38] *SRI*, 127 F.3d at 1470, 44 USPQ2d at 1428.

[39] *Id.*, 44 USPQ2d at 1428.

[40] *Minks*, 546 F.3d at 1376, 89 USPQ2d at 1111 (citing *SRI* and quoting Gart v. Logitech, Inc., 254 F.3d 1334, 1345, 59 USPQ2d 1290, 1298 (Fed. Cir. 2001)).

[41] 35 U.S.C. §101.

[42] Diamond v. Chakrabarty, 447 U.S. 303, 309, 206 USPQ 193, 197 (1980) (quoting S. REP. No. 82-79, at 5 (1952); H.R. REP. No. 82-1923, at 6 (1952)).

[43] Mackay Radio & Tel. Co. v. Radio Corp. of Am., 306 U.S. 86, 94, 40 USPQ 199, 203 (1939).

[44] Rubber-Tip Pencil Co. v. Howard, 87 U.S. 498, 507 (1874).

"A principle, in the abstract, is a fundamental truth; an original cause; a motive; these cannot be patented, as no one can claim in either of them an exclusive right."[45] "Phenomena of nature, though just discovered, mental processes, and abstract intellectual concepts are not patentable, as they are the basic tools of scientific and technological work."[46]

In 1998, the Federal Circuit decided *State Street Bank & Trust Co. v. Signature Financial Group, Inc.*[47] In order to determine whether a claim drawn toward "[a] data processing system for managing a financial services configuration of a portfolio established as a partnership"[48] included patentable subject matter. In this case, the Federal Circuit held that a claimed invention was eligible for patent protection if it involved "some type of practical application, i.e., a 'useful, concrete, and tangible result.'"[49] In 2008, the Federal Circuit revisited Section 101 in *In re Bilski*[50] and held that the machine-or-transformation test is the applicable test for patent-eligible subject matter,[51] and stated that the test in *State Street* should no longer be relied upon.[52] The Supreme Court granted certiorari on *In re Bilski* and in 2010 held that the machine-or-transformation test is not the sole test for determining the patent eligibility of a process, but rather "a useful and important clue, an investigative tool, for determining whether some claimed inventions are processes under §101."[53]

In applying the Supreme Court holding in *Bilski*, the Federal Circuit reasoned that a claim drawn toward "a method for verifying the validity of a credit card transaction over the Internet" was capable of being performed mentally and that "a method that can be performed by human thought alone is merely an abstract idea and is not patent-eligible under §101."[54]

Most recently, the Supreme Court held in *Mayo Collaborative Services v. Prometheus Laboratories, Inc.*[55] that "we have neither said nor implied that the [machine-or-transformation] test trumps the 'law of nature' exclusion."[56] Theoretically, even if a claim satisfies the machine-or-transformation test, it could still be deemed unpatentable subject matter under the law-of-nature exclusion.

---

[45] Le Roy v. Tatham, 55 U.S. 156, 175 (1853).

[46] Gottschalk v. Benson, 409 U.S. 63, 67, 175 USPQ 673, 675 (1972).

[47] 149 F.3d 1368, 47 USPQ2d 1596 (Fed. Cir. 1998).

[48] *Id.* at 1371, 47 USPQ2d at 1599 (Fed. Cir. 1998).

[49] *Id.* at 1373, 47 USPQ2d at 1600–01 (quoting *In re* Alappat, 33 F.3d 1526, 1544, 31 USPQ2d 1545, 1557 (Fed. Cir. 1994)).

[50] 545 F.3d 943, 88 USPQ2d 1385 (Fed. Cir. 2008).

[51] *Id.* at 961, 88 USPQ2d at 1396.

[52] *Id.* at 991, 88 USPQ2d at 1418–19.

[53] Bilski v. Kappos, 130 S. Ct. 3218, 3227, 177 L. Ed. 2d 792, 803, 95 USPQ2d 1001, 1007 (2010).

[54] CyberSource Corp. v. Retail Decisions, Inc., 654 F.3d 1366, 1373, 99 USPQ2d 1690, 1696 (Fed. Cir. 2011).

[55] 132 S. Ct. 1289, 182 L. Ed. 2d 321, 101 USPQ2d 1961 (2012).

[56] *Id.* at 1303, 182 L. Ed. 2d at 337, 101 USPQ2d at 1972.

F. Conclusion and Application of Recent Decisions to the Role of the Jury

[Replace the second paragraph with the following.]

This uncertainty benefits the patent troll that deals with the aggregate result, since the patent troll doesn't usually care which of the ten defendants it sues is ultimately liable for patent infringement, especially if the other nine settle. And since the existence of a jury makes determination of liability and damages hard to predict, a company wary of being found liable for high damages by a patent troll is inclined to settle. To help ameliorate this risk, federal judges have assumed certain responsibilities at trial to help guide jurors to come to the right decision: claim construction is considered a strictly legal concept, and juries are told what the claim terms mean; restrictions about damages, including that the plaintiff must provide actual evidence of damages and irreparable harm to obtain an injunction; restrictions to damage calculation theories such as the abandonment of the 25 percent rule of thumb and the entire market value rule; the creation of a number of legal doctrines (such as ensnarement, and the all elements rule) to minimize the jury's ability to find infringement through the doctrine of equivalents; removal of assumptions the jury could make about negligence as it applies to willful infringement; increased deference of courts to stay cases being reexamined at the USPTO, etc.

In *Markman v. Westview Instruments, Inc.*,[57] the Supreme Court held that requiring the court, rather than the jury, to construe and determine the scope of patent claims did not violate Seventh Amendment right to jury trial. Also, when the meaning of technologic terms and words of arts as used in a particular patent is a question of law and not of fact, the jury is removed from the determination process. However, if extensive evidence related to the meaning and scope of technologic or scientific terms or words of art is disputed, then an underlying factual question arises that a jury may decide.[58]

Following the Federal Rules of Civil Procedure 49, in a jury trial the court "may require the jury to return a special verdict in the form of a special written finding on each issue of fact."[59] The Supreme Court has endorsed and encouraged the use of special verdict interrogatories as "very useful in facilitating review, uniformity, and possibly postverdict judgments as a matter of law."[60] The Federal Circuit strongly recommends use of these techniques, especially in complex cases.[61]

---

[57] 517 U.S. 370, 38 USPQ2d 1461 (1996).

[58] *Id.*

[59] Fed. R. Civ. P. 49(1).

[60] Warner-Jenkinson Co. v. Hilton Davis Chem. Co., 520 U.S. 17, 39 n.8, 41 USPQ2d 1865, 1875 n.8 (1997).

[61] *See* Richardson-Vicks, Inc. v. Upjohn Co., 122 F.3d 1476, 44 USPQ2d 1181 (Fed. Cir. 1997).

The role of the trial court in a patent jury trial is not significantly different from its role in a patent bench trial with respect to legal issues. The Federal Circuit applies the same standard of review, therefore, to legal conclusions on issues such as patent validity. Thus, the Federal Circuit's duty to be satisfied that the law has been correctly applied to the facts is the same regardless of whether a judge or a jury determines those facts.[62]

When one considers the changes made to patent law over the past ten years, one strains to think of any recent jurisprudence that placed more responsibility into the jurists' hands. And that probably makes sense, because jury trials were created so that a panel of one's peers could judge who was wrong and who was right. Since most jurists sitting on a panel in a dispute between a large company and a patent troll are hardly "peers," to the patent troll or the company, what benefit do they even serve aside from adding more uncertainty to the outcome? Perhaps that's why the Federal Circuit and Supreme Court have seen it fit to limit their discretion in patent cases.

[Add the following new sections.]

G. NPE Standing [New Topic]

Non-practicing entities (NPEs) face unique challenges to standing as they typically acquire rights from third parties rather than create and patent their own inventions. Typically, patent rights are assigned to the NPE outright, or the NPE is granted an exclusive license to the patent. The grants in the license will largely determine whether the NPE has proper standing to bring suit. However, most NPEs are sophisticated enough to understand which rights they must acquire in order to gain standing to monetize the patent.

The Patent Act provides that "[a] patentee shall have remedy by civil action for infringement of his patent."[63] The term "patentee" comprises "not only the patentee to whom the patent was issued but also the successors in title to the patentee."[64] However, if the patentee transfers all substantial rights under the patent, it amounts to an assignment and the assignee may be deemed the effective patentee under 35 U.S.C. §281 for purposes of holding constitutional standing to sue another for patent infringement in its own name.[65]

Under 35 U.S.C. §100, "the owner of a patent or the owner's assignee can commence an action for patent infringement, but a licensee alone

---

[62] *See* Lough v. Brunswick Corp., 86 F.3d 1113, 1119, 39 USPQ2d 1100, 1103 (Fed. Cir. 1996).

[63] 35 U.S.C. §281.

[64] 35 U.S.C. §100(d).

[65] Prima Tek II, L.L.C. v. A-Roo Co., 222 F.3d 1372, 1377, 55 USPQ2d 1742, 1745 (Fed. Cir. 2000); *see also* 35 U.S.C. §261; Waterman v. Mackenzie, 138 U.S. 252, 256 (1891); Ortho Pharm. Corp. v. Genetics Inst., Inc., 52 F.3d 1026, 1030, 34 USPQ2d 1444, 1446–47 (Fed. Cir. 1995).

cannot, unless the licensee holds 'all substantial rights' in the patent."[66] A nonexclusive license confers no constitutional standing on the licensee to bring suit or even to join a suit with the patentee because a nonexclusive licensee suffers no legal injury from infringement.[67] An exclusive licensee receives more rights than a nonexclusive licensee, but fewer than an assignee. An example of an exclusive license is a license that grants the exclusive right to practice an invention, but only within a given limited territory.[68]

While a licensee normally does not have standing to sue without the joinder of the patentee (to prevent multiplicity of litigation), an exclusive license may be treated as an assignment for purposes of creating standing if it conveys to the licensee all substantial rights.[69] The Federal Circuit has held that "where the patentee makes an assignment of all substantial rights under the patent," licensee or assignee "may be deemed the effective 'patentee' under 35 U.S.C. §281."[70] Each license and assignment is unique. Therefore, a court "must ascertain the intention of the parties and examine the substance of what [the licensing agreement] granted" to determine if it conveys all substantial rights in the patent and is sufficient to grant standing to the licensee.[71]

Unlike an assignee who may sue in its own name, an exclusive licensee having fewer than all substantial patent rights and seeking to enforce its rights in a patent generally must sue jointly with the patent owner.[72]

A transfer in which the patent owner retained the right to veto sublicenses, the right to patent the invention in other countries, the reversionary right to the patent in case of bankruptcy, and the right to any damages from infringement litigation was held to be a transfer of all substantial rights to a patent as "none of these reserved rights was so substantial as to reduce the transfer to a mere license or indicate an intent not to transfer all substantial rights."[73] In *Vaupel* the plaintiff had been transferred all rights to make, have made, use, sell, lease, rebuild, and sue for patent infringement for '650 Patent. The court held "particularly dispositive" the transfer of the right to sue for patent infringement with the sole requirement that the plaintiff notify the patent owner of such litigation to its conclusion that the plaintiff held all substantial rights.[74]

---

[66]Sicom Sys. Ltd. v. Agilent Techs., Inc., 427 F.3d 971, 976, 76 USPQ2d 1933, 1937 (Fed. Cir. 2005) (citations omitted).

[67]*Ortho Pharm.*, 52 F.3d at 1031, 34 USPQ2d at 1447.

[68]Rite-Hite Corp. v. Kelley Co., 56 F.3d 1538, 1552, 35 USPQ2d 1065, 1074 (Fed. Cir. 1995) (citing Independent Wireless Tel. Co. v. Radio Corp. of Am., 269 U.S. 459, 468–69 (1926)).

[69]*Prima Tek II*, 222 F.3d at 1377–78, 55 USPQ2d at 1746; Vaupel Textilmaschinen KG v. Meccanica Euro Italia S.P.A., 944 F.2d 870, 875, 20 USPQ2d 1045, 1049 (Fed. Cir. 1991).

[70]*Prima Tek II*, 222 F.3d at 1377, 55 USPQ2d at 1746.

[71]*Id.* at 1378, 55 USPQ2d at 1746.

[72]*Ortho Pharm.*, 52 F.3d at 1030, 34 USPQ2d at 1447; *see also* Calgon Corp. v. Nalco Chem. Co., 726 F. Supp. 983, 985, 13 USPQ2d 1529, 1530 ("[T]he patent holder or assignee is a necessary party to an infringement action in order to achieve consistency of interpretation and to avoid multiplicity of litigation. Under federal law, the patentee is the real party in interest in such litigation.").

[73]*Vaupel*, 944 F.2d at 874–75, 20 USPQ2d at 1049; *see also* Buckhorn, Inc. v. Orbis Corp., No. 3:08-CV-00459, 2009 U.S. Dist. LEXIS 68298 (S.D. Ohio July 21, 2009).

[74]*Vaupel*, 944 F.2d at 875, 20 USPQ2d at 1049.

H. Party Joinder [New Topic]

The Leahy-Smith America Invents Act ("AIA")[75] made significant changes to patent law in the litigation context on the subject of joinder of multiple defendants. Legislators specifically attempted to address NPEs litigation practices that typically include multiple defendants and, in rare occasions, can include over 100 defendants. The common thread between each of the defendants is the accusation that they infringed a common patent or patents. This advanced the policy argument of judicial economy. For example, instead of having multiple scheduling conferences, multiple Markman hearings, and multiple trials, courts could do each of the aforementioned once, in a single action. This allowed the court to conserve its resources by avoiding similar invalidity considerations and differing claim constructions for the same patent. In an attempt to curtail litigation filings by NPEs, legislators included a party joinder section in the AIA as follows:

> (a) Joinder of accused infringers.—With respect to any civil action arising under any Act of Congress relating to patents, other than an action or trial in which an act of infringement under [35 USC §271(e)(2)] has been pled, parties that are accused infringers may be joined in one action as defendants or counterclaim defendants, or have their actions consolidated for trial, or counterclaim defendants only if—
>
>> (1) any right to relief is asserted against the parties jointly, severally, or in the alternative with respect to or arising out of the same transaction, occurrence, or series of transactions or occurrences relating to the making, using, importing into the United States, offering for sale, or selling of the same accused product or process; and
>>
>> (2) questions of fact common to all defendants or counterclaim defendants will arise in the action.
>
> (b) Allegations insufficient for joinder.—For purposes of this subsection, accused infringers may not be joined in one action as defendants or counterclaim defendants, or have their actions consolidated for trial, based solely on allegations that they each have infringed the patent or patents in suit.
>
> (c) Waiver.—A party that is an accused infringer may waive the limitations set forth in this section with respect to that party.[76]

This statute has the effect of limiting the defendants in a single suit to those entities whose alleged infringement arose out of the same transaction, occurrence, or series of transactions or occurrences. However, there is limited empirical data to make an accurate determination as to whether this provision has had the desired effect.

---

[75] 112 P.L. 29, 125 Stat. 284 (Sept. 16, 2011).

[76] *Id.* §19 (codified at 35 U.S.C. §299) (effective Sept. 16, 2011).

I.   Induced Infringement [New Topic]

1.   *Willful Blindness after Global-Tech [New Topic]*

In *Global-Tech Appliances, Inc. v. SEB S.A.*, the Supreme Court held that active inducement liability under Section 271(b) requires that the defendant have "knowledge of the existence of the patent that is infringed" and "that the induced acts constitute patent infringement."[77] The Court found that circumstantial evidence for proving knowledge under the objective deliberate indifference standard used by the Federal Circuit was not appropriate,[78] but rather that knowledge may be proved circumstantially under the tougher subjective standard of willful blindness.[79]

The standard for willful blindness articulated in *Global-Tech* is "(1) the defendant must subjectively believe that there is a high probability that a fact exists and (2) the defendant must take deliberate actions to avoid learning of that fact."[80] Willful blindness requires more than knowledge of a substantial risk—it requires active efforts to avoid knowledge of the potentially infringing nature of its activities.[81]

When examining the facts of the case, the Court found that the question of whether the induced acts that constituted infringement was not at issue, and further that "there is no need to invoke the doctrine of willful blindness to establish that [defendant] knew that the retailers who purchased its fryer were selling the product in the American market; [defendant] was indisputably aware that its customers were selling its product in this country."[82]

The Court ultimately focused its factual inquiry on the defendant's failure to identify the patent covering the plaintiff's product, finding that the evidence "was more than sufficient for a jury to find that [defendant] subjectively believed that [plaintiff's] fryer was patented, that [defendant] took deliberate steps to avoid knowing that fact, and that it therefore willfully blinded itself to the infringing nature of [the direct infringer's] sales."[83]

Accordingly, the Court's holding can be understood to mean that a defendant can willfully blind itself either to the fact that (1) a patent exists or (2) the conduct that was induced constitutes infringement of that patent. It logically follows that if a defendant's actions amount to willful blindness as to the knowledge that a patent exists, he has also willfully blinded himself as to whether the conduct that was induced would constitute infringement of that patent.

---

[77] Global-Tech Appliances, Inc. v. SEB S.A., 131 S. Ct. 2060, 2068, 179 L. Ed. 2d 1167, 1177, 98 USPQ2d 1665, 1671 (2011).
[78] *Id.*, 179 L. Ed. 2d at 1177, 98 USPQ2d at 1671.
[79] *Id.* at 2068–69, 179 L. Ed. 2d at 1177, 98 USPQ2d at 1671.
[80] *Id.* at 2070, 179 L. Ed. 2d at 1179, 98 USPQ2d at 1672 (footnote omitted).
[81] *Id.* at 2068, 179 L. Ed. 2d at 1177, 98 USPQ2d at 1671.
[82] *Id.* at 2070, 179 L. Ed. 2d at 1178–79, 98 USPQ2d at 1672.
[83] *Id.* at 2072, 179 L. Ed. 2d at 1180, 98 USPQ2d at 1673.

Courts applying willful blindness hold that "defendants cannot escape [liability] by deliberately shielding themselves from clear evidence of critical facts that are strongly suggested by the circumstances."[84] Examples of what has been found to establish willful blindness include a deliberate failure to investigate[85] and a purposeful contrivance to avoid learning of infringing activities.[86]

2. *Direct Infringement After Akamai [New Topic]*

In *Akamai Technologies, Inc. v. Limelight Networks, Inc.*, the Federal Circuit held that a defendant is liable for inducing infringement if it can be shown that (1) it knew of the plaintiff's patent, (2) it induced the performance of the steps of the method claimed in the patent, and (3) those steps were performed.[87] The Federal Circuit clarified that "all the steps of a claimed method must be performed in order to find induced infringement, but that it is not necessary to prove that all the steps were committed by a single entity."[88]

Akamai was heard en banc and decided by the narrowest of margins: 6-5. This ruling is very likely to be granted cert. by the U.S. Supreme Court, as it changes the long-standing law on induced infringement. Prior to *Akamai*, an induced infringement cause of action for a method claim could be brought against a defendant only if the defendant practiced all the elements of the asserted method claim. For now, the defendant need not practice all the steps of an asserted method claim to induce infringement—they need only be practiced in some permutation if the other elements are met.

III. THE LEAHY-SMITH AMERICA INVENTS ACT (PATENT REFORM ACT OF 2011)

[Add the following text at the end of the section.]

Upon its enactment on September 16, 2011, the America Invents Act kicked off a series of new patent rules which take or have taken effect at various dates. An initial set of rules took effect immediately while additional rules took effect ten days and sixty days later. Two additional sets of rules were to take effect twelve months from enactment—September 16, 2012—and eighteen months from enactment—March 16, 2013.

---

[84]*Id.* at 2068–69, 179 L. Ed. 2d at 1177, 98 USPQ2d at 1671.

[85]Hard Rock Café Licensing Corp. v. Concession Servs. Inc., 955 F.2d 1143, 1149, 21 USPQ2d 1764, 1768 (7th Cir. 1992) (trademark infringement).

[86]Tiffany, Inc. v. eBay, Inc., 576 F. Supp. 2d 463, 515 (S.D.N.Y. 2008) (trademark infringement). *See* Coach, Inc. v. Gata Corp., No. 10-cv-141, 2011 U.S. Dist. Lexis 62317, at *18 (D.N.H. June 9, 2011) (quoting *Tiffany*) (trademark infringement).

[87]Akamai Techs., Inc. v. Limelight Networks, Inc., 2012 U.S. App. LEXIS 18532, 50, 2012 WL 3764695 (Fed. Cir. Aug. 31, 2012).

[88]*Id.* at 11–12.

Effective Immediately (September 16, 2011)

Among the set of rules which took effect immediately is a new standard for *inter partes* reexamination which requires a "reasonable likelihood that the petitioner would prevail with respect to at least 1 of the claims challenged in the petition."[89] This new provision is part of Section 6 of the Act, which also eliminates federal court review of USPTO reexaminations.

Also of immediate effect is a new prior "commercial use" defense for accused infringers who can prove they used the patented technology more than one year before the filing date of the claimed invention.[90] Although the defense does not invalidate the claimed patent, it provides the commercial user an escape from liability. This new provision is discussed in Section 5 of the Act, which also defines commercial use.

Perhaps the most relevant new patent rule relating to cyberspace is the virtual Web site marking rule. This new rule, at Section 16 of the Act, effective upon enactment, recognizes links on public Web sites which connect inventions to patent numbers as sufficient public notice of patent protection.[91] Additional provisions which took immediate effect include an end to the "best mode defense" at Section 15[92] and new joinder rules at Section 19(d) aimed at restricting the common patent troll tactic of joining unrelated accused infringers.[93]

Effective 10 Days After Enactment (September 26, 2011)

Ten days after the AIA was enacted, Section 11 added a 15 percent surcharge to all patent fees.[94] This was also the date when the new priority examination option took effect. For $4,800 (or $2,400 for small entities), new applications for non-provisional original utility patents can be put on a new priority track.[95]

Effective 60 Days After Enactment (November 6, 2011)

On November 6, 2011, a new $400 fee took effect ($200 for small entities) under Section 10 for new applications which are not filed online.[96]

Effective 12 Months After Enactment (September 16, 2012)

Two significant changes were to take effect twelve months from enactment—on September 16, 2012. First, new rules limiting post-grant reviews to novelty and nonobviousness challenges take effect under Section 6 of the Act. And as discussed in detail in the main volume,[97] Section 18 of the Act establishes a transitional post-grant review process to test the validity of business-method patents.[98]

---

[89] 112 P.L. 29, 125 Stat. 284, §6(a).
[90] *Id.* §5(a)(2).
[91] *Id.* §16(a)(1).
[92] *Id.* §15(a).
[93] *Id.* §19(d).
[94] *Id.* §11(i)(1).
[95] *Id.* §11(h)(1), (2).
[96] *Id.* §10(h)(1), (b).
[97] *See* Section III.A of the main volume. *See also* Section III.A of this supplement, *infra.*
[98] 112 P.L. 29, 125 Stat. 284, §18.

Another significant change to the patent application process which takes effect at this time is the ability for third-parties to submit prior art references to the USPTO during a patent's initial examination period. This new provision injects an element of "crowdsourcing"[99] into the patent examination process which has proven to help patent examiners to limit testing. USPTO Director, David Kappos, said "allowing the USPTO to harness the Internet and crowdsource the search for additional prior art helps patent examiners widen the scope of their review and offers applicants heightened confidence in the validity of their patents once issued."[100]

Effective 18 Months After Enactment (March 6, 2013)

Perhaps the biggest change to the U.S. patent system will take effect on March 6, 2013, when the system changes from first-to-invent to first-to-file. Patent applications filed on or after this date will be subject to new prior art and disclosure rules according to Section 3 of the Act.[101] Among these new rules is a one-year grace period allowing inventors to file their application within one year of making certain public disclosures. This new provision will replace the current one-year on-sale bar which permits sale of a patented invention only within one year of filing the patent. This section of the Act will also amend the novelty and nonobviousness sections of the Patent Act, 35 U.S.C. §§102, 103 (respectively).

In addition, Section 3 provides new rules enabling a patent owner to bring a "derivation hearing" against another patent owner who claims to have the same invention with an earlier effective filing date.[102] This new rule will replace the current interference proceeding provisions.

A. Business Method Patent Transitional Review

[Add the following text at the end of the section.]

The United State Patent and Trademark Office (USPTO) has published a series of proposed rules implementing the provisions of American Invents Act, including the rule of practice for trials before the Patent Trial and Appeal Board,[103] trial practice guide,[104] rules for *inter partes* review,[105] post-grant review,[106] the transitional program for covered business methods,[107] and the technological invention definition and deriva-

---

[99] *See* Jeff Howe, *The Rise of Crowdsourcing*, WIRED MAGAZINE (*available at* http://www.wired.com/wired/archive/14.06/crowds.html).

[100] David Kappos, *The America Invents Act: A Patent Law Game-Changer*, USPTO (*available at* http://www.uspto.gov/news/speeches/2011/kappos_brookings.jsp).

[101] 112 P.L. 29, 125 Stat. 284, §3.

[102] *Id.* §3(i).

[103] 77 Fed. Reg. 6879 (to be codified at 37 C.F.R. pts. 42, 90) (Feb. 9, 2012).

[104] *Id.* at 6868 (to be codified at 37 C.F.R. pt. 42).

[105] 77 Fed. Reg. 7041 (to be codified at 37 C.F.R. pt. 42) (Feb. 10, 2012).

[106] *Id.* at 7060 (to be codified at 37 C.F.R. pt. 42).

[107] *Id.* at 7080 (to be codified at 37 C.F.R. pt. 42).

tion proceeding,[108] among others. All the proposed rules deserve a close look, especially the trial practice guide, which provides detailed procedural guidance for all the new proceedings, including *inter partes* review, post-grant review, the transitional program for covered business methods, and the derivation proceeding.[109] Here, we focus on the proposed rules regarding the definitions and scopes of "covered business method patent" and "technological invention" for the purpose of the transitional program for covered business method patents under Section 18 of American Invents Act.[110]

The USPTO adopts the definition of "covered business method patent" specified in the American Invents Act as "a patent that claims a method or corresponding apparatus for performing data processing or other operations used in the practice, administration, or management of a financial product or service, except that the term does not include patents for technological inventions."[111] Because this definition fails to provide additional practical guidance, we have to closely examine some key phrases in the definition along the legislative history to determine what patents are considered as covered business method patents.

The "method or corresponding apparatus" in this definition includes, but is not limited to, "any type of claim contained in a patent, including, method claims, system claims, apparatus claims, graphical user interface claims, data structure claims" and "set of instructions on storage media claims."[112] Furthermore, "financial product or service" is a rather broad definition. Senator Schumer has listed numerous types of financial products or services, including, but are not limited to, "extending credit, servicing loans, activities related to extending and accepting credit, leasing of personal or real property, real estate services, appraisals of real or personal property, deposit-taking activities, selling, providing, issuing or accepting stored value or payment instruments, check cashing, collection or processing, financial data processing, administration and processing of benefits, financial fraud detection and prevention, financial advisory or management consulting services, issuing, selling and trading financial instruments and other securities, insurance products and services, collecting, analyzing, maintaining or providing consumer report information or other account information, asset management, trust functions, annuities, securities brokerage, private placement services, investment transactions, and related support services."[113] Clearly, the targets of the business method patent transitional review are not limited to financial service companies. Any company providing a broadly defined financial product or service faces the risk as well.

---

[108] *Id.* at 7095 (to be codified at 37 C.F.R. pt. 42).

[109] 77 Fed. Reg. 6868 (to be codified at 37 C.F.R. pt. 42) (Feb. 9, 2012).

[110] 112 P.L. 29, 125 Stat. 284, §18 (effective Sept. 16, 2012).

[111] Proposed 37 C.F.R. 42.301(a).

[112] 157 Cong. Rec. S1364 (daily ed. Mar. 8, 2011) (statement of Sen. Schumer).

[113] *Id.* at S5432 (daily ed. Sept. 8, 2011) (statement of Sen. Schumer).

Despite the broad interpretation of "financial product or service," the scope of patents eligible for transitional review is even broader. It is not limited to patents directly covering a specific financial product or service[114]; any ancillary activities related to a financial product or service may render a patent as a "covered business method patent." Such activities include, but are not limited to, "marketing, customer interfaces, Web site management and functionality, transmission or management of data, servicing, underwriting, customer communications, and back office operations."[115] So long as the patent could be applied to a financial produce or service, the patent would be deemed to cover a "financial product or service,"[116] thus, qualify as a "covered business method patent." Also, a patent holder would hardly avoid transitional review if the holder alleges a patent infringement by a financial product or service, because the patent would be deemed to cover a "financial product or service," even if the asserted claims do not specially reference to a financial produce or service.[117]

Given the broad scope of covered business method patents, it would be difficult for patent applicants to avoid transitional review by a clever drafting, unless they can demonstrate that the patent is for a "technological invention." However, the definition of "technological invention" proposed by USPTO is somewhat vague. According to the proposed rules, in order to determine whether a patent is for a "technological invention," it "will be considered on a case-by-case basis: whether the claimed subject matter as a whole recites a technological feature that is novel and unobvious over the prior art; and solves a technical problem using a technical solution."[118] Public comments about the vague definitions of "technological feature" "technical problem," and "technical solution" allege that most computer-based inventions are potentially "technical," thus this definition would exclude most computer-based patents from the scope of "covered business method patents."[119] So far, the USPTO expresses no intent to define the above terms, but emphasizes that all the determinations will be conducted on a case-by-case basis.[120] However, legislative history does make it clear that a patent is not exempted from transitional review merely because it recites technology.[121] Among others things, the patent's novelty must turn on a technological innovation over the prior art. A patent is not excluded as a "technological invention" if the patent uses known technology to accomplish a business process or method of conducting business, even if the process or method is novel.[122]

---

[114]*Id.* at S1365 (daily ed. Mar. 8, 2011) (statement of Sen. Schumer).

[115]*Id.*

[116]*Id.*

[117]*Id.*

[118]Proposed 37 C.F.R. 42.301(b).

[119]American Invents Act Roadshow Video, "Board: Specific Rules for Post Grant Review, Inter Partes Review, Covered Business Method Review, and Derivation," USPTO (*available at* http://www.uspto.gov/aia_implementation/index.jsp).

[120]*Id.*

[121]157 Cong. Rec. S1364 (daily ed. Mar. 8, 2011) (statement of Sen. Schumer).

[122]*Id.*

Covered business method patents under Section 18 encompass a broad range of patents with a narrow "technological invention" exception. It remains to be seen if additional guidance will be provided by the USPTO.

PART IV

ISSUES ARISING FROM CONDUCTING BUSINESS ONLINE

11
Trade Secrets Online

There have been no significant changes or developments in the law relevant to this chapter since the publication of the main volume.

12

Personal Jurisdiction and the Internet*

Andrew N. Stein
DLA Piper LLP (US)
Washington, D.C.

Mansi H. Shah
Morgan, Lewis & Bockius LLP
Chicago, Illinois

Archit P. Shah
Kirkland & Ellis LLP
Chicago, Illinois

*The authors wish to thank Rebecca Stephens, a 2012 summer associate in the Chicago office of Morgan, Lewis & Bockius LLP, for her assistance with this supplement.

III. Personal Jurisdiction Through Internet Activity in the United States

[Add the following new section.]

B. Criticism of the *Zippo* Test [New Topic]

Some courts have identified several downsides of the *Zippo* test and its "slippery slope."[1] One critique of the *Zippo* test is that it is too "mechanical" and formulaic a test when Supreme Court precedent has disfavored "talismanic jurisdictional formulas."[2] In addition, it can be difficult to

---

[1] *See* Caiazzo v. American Royal Arts Corp., 73 So. 3d 245, 255–56 (Fla. Dist. Ct. App. 2011). *See also* Hy Cite Corp. v. Badbusinessbureau.com, LLC, 297 F. Supp. 2d 1154, 70 USPQ2d 1266 (W.D. Wis. 2004).

[2] *Caiazzo*, 73 So. 2d at 255 (citing Burger King v. Rudzewicz, 471 U.S. 462, 478, 485 (1985)).

classify a Web site into one category or the other, and even if a Web site can be properly classified, the site owner's intent may be more relevant than the site's capabilities to the determination of jurisdiction.[3] Finally, the *Zippo* test does not take into consideration other elements of personal jurisdiction such as the nexus between the Web site and the cause of action or the nature of the contacts through the Web site; removing these elements from the analysis may lead to erroneous results.[4]

[Revise the Section IV heading to read as follows.]

IV. SURVEY OF INTERNET JURISDICTION CASES [REVISED HEADING]

A. First Circuit

[Add the following text at the end of the section.]

Perhaps evidencing a lower bar for Web site-based jurisdiction in the First Circuit, the court in *Henderson v. Laser Spine Institute LLC*[5] found that when the purpose of a Web site, as a whole, is "commercial" and "not merely educational" in nature, personal jurisdiction may lie.[6] In this case, the Laser Spine Institute, a Florida company, "operated a website aimed at bringing in patients from other states" and the court found that the site was "more than a passive website containing information that is just accessible for viewing by users in other states."[7] Indeed, the "LSI website provides a form to schedule a free MRI review which may be submitted online, as well as online contact request forms that prompt return calls from the company."[8] The court concluded that "[b]ecause the District of Maine has not adopted the *Zippo* test, a broader look at the Defendants' use of the internet in their purposeful availment of Maine customers" was appropriate and found that LSI's "website campaign, like their national print marketing, is intended to reach a large national audience, including potential customers in Maine" and, as a result, Laser Spine "successfully exploited at least part of the Maine market" in such a way that it could reasonably expect to be haled into court there.[9]

---

[3] *Hy Cite Corp.*, 297 F. Supp. 2d at 1160, 70 USPQ2d at 1270–71.

[4] *Id.*, 70 USPQ2d at 1271.

[5] 815 F. Supp. 2d 353 (D. Me. 2011).

[6] *Id.* at 376–77 (D. Me. 2011); *see also* Edvisors Network, Inc. v. Educational Advisors, Inc., 755 F. Supp. 2d. 272, 282–83 (D. Mass. 2010) (finding personal jurisdiction where Educational Advisors' Web site was "not simply passive" and but provided "a means for reaching out to attract new business from foreign residents, including those in Massachusetts" and defendant took actions to encourage contacts in the forum state).

[7] *Henderson*, 815 F. Supp. 2d at 376–77.

[8] *Id.* at 377.

[9] *Id.*

G. Seventh Circuit

[Add the following text at the end of the section.]

The Seventh Circuit's aversion to the *Zippo* test was reaffirmed in *Collazo v. Enterprise Holdings, Inc.*[10] Collazo's claims arose out of a trolley accident in Puerto Rico in which she was riding a trolley from the airport to Enterprise's car rental terminal.[11] During this trolley ride, Collazo, an Indiana citizen, was ejected from her seat after a sudden stop.[12] Collazo sued Enterprise, a Missouri corporation, and Prerac, a Puerto Rico corporation, in the Northern District of Indiana.[13] Both defendants moved to dismiss for lack of personal jurisdiction.[14] In response, Collazo argued that the defendants were subject to general personal jurisdiction on the basis of the "interactivity" of their Web sites, which were both accessible in Indiana.[15] After reconfirming that the Seventh Circuit does not apply the *Zippo* test in which the interactivity of a Web site bears on the personal jurisdiction question,[16] the court stated that the "proper jurisdictional test for Internet-based cases is instead a matter of determining whether a defendant has established sufficient minimum contacts with a forum to justify the exercise of personal jurisdiction over it in the forum state."[17] The court found that even though Indiana residents could make reservations to rent vehicles through Enterprise's Web site and could search for employment opportunities through Prerac's Web site, so could "residents of any state in the U.S., as well as citizens in Canada, Ireland, Germany and the U.K.,"[18] this was not enough: "no matter how interactive Defendants' websites may be, Defendants' maintenance of those sites, alone, does not approach the level of 'continuous and systematic' contacts necessary to establish general personal jurisdiction."[19]

M. Federal Circuit

[Add the following text at the end of the section.]

With *Trintec* as a backdrop for personal jurisdiction issues, the court in *Original Creations, Inc. v. Ready America, Inc.*[20] considered whether con-

---

[10] 823 F. Supp. 2d 865 (N.D. Ind. 2011).

[11] *Id.* at 867.

[12] *Id.*

[13] *Id.*

[14] *Id.*

[15] *Id.*

[16] *Id.* at 869.

[17] *Id.*

[18] *Id.* at 870. "And, tellingly, Collazo never contends that she made any reservations through either of these sites. Nor does she contend that consumers generally can make payments for goods or services, or enter into contracts with Defendants, through either of these sites." *Id.*

[19] *Id.*

[20] 836 F. Supp. 2d 711 (N.D. Ill. 2011).

tacts through defendant Life+Gear's Web site were sufficient for personal jurisdiction. and applied the law of the regional circuit, in this case, the Seventh Circuit.[21] Life+Gear operated a Web site through which customers could place orders for products that allegedly infringed Original Creations' patents.[22] However, the "interactive" order functionality of Life+Gear's Web site was provided by a third-party, Yahoo!, and on this basis, Life+Gear argued that its Web site was merely "passive."[23] Who supplied the interactive functionality on the Web site mattered none to Judge Bucklo's jurisdictional analysis, however: "In the case before me, [Original Creations] has documented one sale made to an Illinois resident, plaintiff himself, via the Life+Gear website.... That sale alone is an insufficient base upon which to find personal jurisdiction."[24]

V. INTERNET JURISDICTION AFTER *ZIPPO*

[Add the following new section.]

D.   Peer-to-Peer File Sharing Protocols [New Topic]

Like virtual worlds, interesting jurisdictional issues surround cases involving peer-to-peer file sharing protocols. "BitTorrent" is one of the most popular peer-to-peer file sharing protocols. And unsurprisingly litigation has followed: "[i]n the last few years, copyright litigation involving BitTorrent file-sharing protocol has proliferated ...."[25]

The Northern District of California described the BitTorrent file sharing protocol:

> The BitTorrent protocol operates as follows. First, a user locates a small "torrent" file. This file contains information about the files to be shared and about the tracker, the computer that coordinates the file distribution. Second, the user loads the torrent file into a BitTorrent client, which automatically attempts to connect to the tracker listed in the torrent file. Third, the tracker responds with a list of peers and the BitTorrent client connects to those peers to begin downloading data from and distributing data to the other peers in the swarm. When the download is complete, the BitTorrent client continues distributing data to the peers in the swarm until the user manually disconnects form [*sic*] the swarm or the BitTorrent client otherwise does the same.[26]

---

[21]*Id.* at 713 ("[W]here the Federal Circuit has not addressed a specific issue regarding personal jurisdiction in Illinois, I look to Seventh Circuit law as persuasive authority.").

[22]*Id.* at 714.

[23]*Id.* "The distinction between Life+Gear and the Yahoo! Store ... seems to be one without a difference, since sales are initiated through the Life+Gear website and processed by Life+Gear." *Id.* at 715.

[24]*Id.* at 716.

[25]Digital Sin, Inc. v. Does 1-27, No. 12-cv-3873, 2012 WL 2036035, at *2, 2012 U.S. Dist. LEXIS 78832, at *5. (S.D.N.Y. June 6, 2012).

[26]Diabolic Video Prods. v. Does 1-2099, No. 10-cv-5865, 2011 WL 3100404, *2, 2011 U.S. Dist. LEXIS 58351, at *3–4 (N.D. Cal. May 31, 2011).

Accordingly, many different parts of one particular file may be down-loaded from many different computers in many different jurisdictions. Answering the question of which court has jurisdiction over claims concerning the downloading of that file (e.g., copyright infringement) becomes decidedly muddy. A few courts have recently addressed this issue.

Many of these decisions in these "BitTorrent" cases have focused on the propriety of the Rule 45 subpoena used to determine the identities behind the particular computer Internet Protocol ("IP") addresses. However, some have gone farther and have addressed more substantive jurisdictional issues.

Before particular defendants have been identified, "most courts have held that a plaintiff succeeds in making out a *prima facie* case of personal jurisdiction where, relying on geolocation software that can identify the likely geographical locations of IP addresses, the plaintiff alleges that all defendants reside in the state within which the court is located."[27]

Once particular defendants have been identified as more than just an IP address, courts have been able to conduct a more substantive personal jurisdiction analysis. For example, in *Liberty Media Holdings, LLC v. Tabora*,[28] the defendants were accused of republishing and distributing copies of Liberty Media's copyrighted work to "at least 840 other individuals over the Internet, including 136 residents of California" through the BitTorrent protocol.[29]

Defendant Tabora filed a motion to dismiss for lack of personal jurisdiction and argued that the Southern District of California did not have jurisdiction over him because he did not have sufficient knowledge of Liberty Media's San Diego location and participating in a BitTorrent "swarm" was insufficient to confer personal jurisdiction.[30] Liberty Media argued in response that specific jurisdiction existed in the Southern District court because Tabora distributed the copyrighted work to California and Tabora knew that these acts of alleged infringement would cause harm in San Diego (where Liberty Media was headquartered), and that jurisdiction in San Diego was reasonable.[31]

---

[27] *Digital Sin, Inc.*, 2012 WL 2036035, at *3, 2012 U.S. Dist. LEXIS 78832, at *8; *see also, e.g.*, Digital Sins, Inc. v. John Does 1-245, No. 11-cv-8170, 2012 WL 1744838, 2012 U.S. Dist. LEXIS 69286 (S.D.N.Y. May 15, 2012).

[28] No. 11-cv-651, 2012 WL 28788, 2012 U.S. Dist. LEXIS 1101 (S.D. Cal. Jan. 4, 2012).

[29] *Id.* at *1, 2012 U.S. Dist. LEXIS 1101, at *2 ; *see also, e.g.*, Malibu Media, LLC v. John Does 1-35, No. 12-cv-1135, 2012 WL 2502710, 2012 U.S. Dist. LEXIS 89946 (S.D. Cal. June 28, 2012); DigiProtect USA Corp. v. John/Jane Does 1-240, No. 10-cv-8760, 2011 WL 4444666, 2011 U.S. Dist. LEXIS 109464 (S.D.N.Y. Sept. 26, 2011) (rejecting personal jurisdiction over defendants located around the United States based solely on the ground that they participated in a swarm with a subset of other defendants that resided in the forum state); DigiProtect USA Corp. v. John/Jane Does 1-266, No. 10-cv-8759, 2011 WL 1466073, 2011 U.S. Dist. LEXIS 40679 (S.D.N.Y. Apr. 13, 2011) ("no showing that any of the Doe defendants expected or reasonably should have expected their downloading of this film [via peer-to-peer file sharing network] to have consequences in New York" and plaintiff could only serve subpoenas on ISP accounts located in New York).

[30] *Liberty Media*, 2012 WL 28788, at *2, 2012 U.S. Dist. LEXIS 1101, at *7.

[31] *Id.* at *1, 2012 U.S. Dist. LEXIS 1101, at *4.

Applying the *Calder* effects test, the court concluded that it did not have personal jurisdiction in the Southern District of California over Liberty Media's claims against Tabora.[32] In particular, the court found that the second (express aiming) and third (foreseeability of harm) prongs of this test were not met in this case.[33] With respect to the express aiming requirement, Liberty Media argued that Tabora expressly aimed his conduct at the Southern District forum because his participation in the swarm "resulted in [Liberty Media's] work being downloaded by users in California."[34] The court found this argument unpersuasive: "Because every user simultaneously receives and transfers information to the other users in the swarm, a participant in the swarm has no control over where he distributes the information" to the other users.[35] "Where the files get distributed to is controlled by the location of the other participants in the swarm, not by the distributor's conduct."[36] As a result, the court dismissed Liberty Media's claims due to lack of personal jurisdiction.[37]

---

[32] *Id.* at *7, 2012 U.S. Dist. LEXIS 1101, at *23–24.
[33] *Id.* at *2–6, 2012 U.S. Dist. LEXIS 1101, at *9–21.
[34] *Id.* at *3, 2012 U.S. Dist. LEXIS 1101, at *10.
[35] *Id.*, 2012 U.S. Dist. LEXIS 1101, at *11.
[36] *Id.*, 2012 U.S. Dist. LEXIS 1101, at *11
[37] *Id.* at *10, 2012 U.S. Dist. LEXIS 1101, at *30.

13

Intellectual Property Issues Raised by Email

Michael B. Smith
Sony Computer Entertainment America
Foster City, California

Sara Anne Hook
Indiana University School of Informatics
Indianapolis, Indiana

Aly Dossa
Osha Liang LLP
Houston, Texas

II. Issues Arising Out of Permissible Use of Email

A. Privacy/Confidentiality

[Add the following text at the end of the section.]

Two recent pieces of legislation have been introduced in Congress that reflect growing concerns over what should be considered permissible with respect to accessing a person's email. First, HR. 3991, the Keep Employees' Emails and Phones Secure Act (KEEP Secure Act), which was introduced on February 9, 2012, would amend the National Labor Relations Act to prohibit the National Labor Relations Board (NLRB) from requiring an employer to provide the NLRB or a labor organization with an employee's telephone number or email address.[1] A second bill, H.R. 5050, the Social Networking Online Protection Act, which was introduced

---

[1]H.R. 3991, 112th Cong. (2012), *available at* Keep Employees' Emails and Phones Secure Act (KEEP Secure Act), *available at* http://thomas.loc.gov/cgi-bin/query/z?c112:H.R.3991 (last visited September 11, 2012).

on April 27, 2012, primarily addresses the recent requests by employers to obtain user names and passwords to social media sites such as Facebook from employees or from job applicants as part of the interviewing process.[2] Note that the language also references attempts to require, request or access private email accounts from employees and job applicants. The bill summary notes that the Act

> Prohibits employers from: (1) requiring or requesting that an employee or applicant for employment provide a user name, password, or any other means for accessing a private *email* account or personal account on a social networking website; or (2) discharging, disciplining, discriminating against, denying employment or promotion to, or threatening to take any such action against any employee or applicant who refuses to provide such information, files a compliant [*sic*] or institutes a proceeding under this Act, or testifies in any such proceeding.[3]

An additional provision in the proposed legislation noted in the summary would amend the Higher Education Act of 1965 and the Elementary and Secondary Education Act of 1965 "to prohibit certain institutions of higher education and local educational agencies from requesting such password or account information from students or potential students."[4] The bill also forbids a variety of retaliatory actions against employees, applicants, students and potential students who refuse to provide the information or who seek redress through filing a complaint, instituting a proceeding or testifying in a proceeding.[5] Both civil penalties and injunctive relief would be available.[6]

1. Work vs. Home

[Add the following text at the end of the section.]

A new book by Nelson, Ries, and Simek provides a chapter on email security, along with substantial information on securing all types of devices.[7]

2. Document Retention Policies

[Add the following text at the end of the section.]

---

[2]H.R.5050, 112th Cong. (2012), *available at* http://thomas.loc.gov/cgi-bin/query/z?c112:H.R.5050 (last visited September 11, 2012).

[3]Bill Summary & Status, 112th Cong. (2011-2012), H.R. 5050: CRS Summary, *available at* http://thomas.loc.gov/cgi-bin/bdquery/z?d112:HR05050:@@@D&summ2=m& (emphasis added).

[4]*Id.*

[5]H.R.5050, 112th Cong. (2012) §2(a)(2).

[6]*Id.* §2(b)(1).

[7]SHARON D. NELSON, DAVID G. RIES & JOHN W. SIMEK, LOCKED DOWN: INFORMATION SECURITY FOR LAWYERS (ABA 2012).

A recent article by Nelson and Simek outlines a number of polices and plans that firms should have in place to deal with the vast amount of electronic information that is being generated by employees using a variety of devices and social media sites.[8] These same suggestions seem appropriate for any corporation or organization and the authors also note the importance of annual training as a way to reinforce these policies and plans. Among the policies that the authors advocate for law firms that encompass email and other popular forms of electronic communication and that pose risks to client confidentiality are an electronic communications and Internet use policy, a social media policy, a document retention policy, a secure password policy, an equipment disposal policy, and policies for mobile security.

The technology plans that Nelson and Simek consider essential for law firms are an incident response plan, a disaster recovery plan, and a litigation hold plan. The authors note that "[t]hese policies and plans are an integral part of risk management and ensuring business continuity, two things near and dear to the heart of all lawyers."[9] Drawing on the work of Nelson and Simek, Kerschberg also discusses why companies should have robust social media policies and a secure and reliable method for archiving information generated through social media, especially since it is discoverable in litigation.[10]

B. Discovery

1. Attorney-Client Privilege

[Add the following text at the end of the section.]

Since July 2011, a number of cases have addressed the issue of privilege for email that was requested as part of the discovery process. These cases suggest that courts are becoming more comfortable within the realm of electronic discovery and the responsibilities of clients and counsel for preservation and production of electronically stored information and less patient when the appropriate steps and safeguards are not in place, especially with respect to privilege.

Another theme of some of the cases is the failure of the party or its counsel to address inadvertent disclosure in a timely manner. For example, in *Ceglia v. Zuckerberg*,[11] the court held that the attorney-client privilege

---

[8]Sharon D. Nelson & John W. Simek. *Essential Law Firm Technology Policies and Plans* (Sensei Enters., Inc. 2012), *available at* http://www.senseient.com/articles/pdf/Essential_Law_Firm_Policies_and_Plans.pdf (last visited June 28, 2012).

[9]*Id.* at 5.

[10]Ben Kerschberg, *Managing Information Risk and Archiving Social Media* (Forbes 9/28/2011), *available at* http://www.forbes.com/sites/benkerschberg/2011/09/28/managing-information-risk-and-archiving-social-media/ (last visited June 28, 2012).

[11]No. 10-CV-00569A(F), 2012 WL 1392965, 2012 U.S. Dist. LEXIS 55367 (W.D.N.Y. Apr. 19, 2012).

was waived when an email was inadvertently produced by an information technology expert. The court found that the plaintiff and counsel did not take reasonable steps to prevent disclosure of the email nor did they act promptly to address this lapse once it was discovered, waiting nearly two months after the material was disseminated to request that it be returned or destroyed.[12] In *Williams v. District of Columbia*,[13] the court denied the defendant's motion to exclude an inadvertently produced email because the defendant failed to satisfy the burden of establishing that reasonable steps were taken to prevent disclosure and did not promptly take steps to rectify the error.[14]

Courts are also finding that privilege has been waived when parties do not take reasonable to preserve confidentiality. For example, in *Pacific Coast Steel, Inc. v. Leany*,[15] the plaintiff had purchased the assets of several companies in which the defendant had an ownership interest and became a high-level employee. He was later terminated and his computer was seized. PCS claimed that Leany had been previously informed that the computer was the property of PCS, that all documents would be merged into a single PCS server and that PCS reserved the right to monitor the use of the computer system. Nevertheless, he made no effort to remove any confidential or privileged information during an email migration or upon being terminated. In particular, the court noted that Leany could not have had any expectation of privacy in the emails.[16] This case especially useful because it points to the dangers of waiving privilege for otherwise confidential information when using an employer-provided computer to communicate with accountants, spouses or attorneys if the employer has reserved the right to monitor usage and has an Acceptable Use Policy for email and other electronic communications systems. The ABA's Formal Opinion 11-459, August 4, 2011, Duty to Protect the Con-

---

[12] *Id. See* Electronic Discovery Law, Expert's Inadvertent Production Results in Waiver of Privilege Absent Sufficient Supervision by Counsel or Prompt Steps to Rectify Disclosure, *available at* http://www.ediscoverylaw.com/2012/05/articles/case-summaries/experts-inadvertent-production-results-in-waiver-of-privilege-absent-sufficient-supervision-by-counsel-or-prompt-steps-to-rectify-disclosure/ (K&L Gates May 24, 2012) (last visited June 28, 2012).

[13] 806 F. Supp. 2d 44 (D.D.C. 2011). *See* Electronic Discovery Law, Court Denies Motion to Exclude Inadvertently Produced Email, Rejects Argument that 26(b)(5)(B) Request for the Email's Return Satisfied FRE 502(b)(3) Obligation, *available at* http://www.ediscoverylaw.com/2011/09/articles/case-summaries/court-denies-motion-to-exclude-inadvertently-produced-email-rejects-argument-that-26b5b-request-for-the-emails-return-satisfied-fre-502b3-obligation/print.html (K&L Gates Sept. 5, 2011) (last visited June 28, 2012).

[14] *Williams v. District of Columbia*, 806 F. Supp. 2d (D.D.C. 2011). (*See* Court Denies Motion to Exclude Inadvertently Produced Email, Rejects Argument that 26(b)(5)(B) Request for the Email's Return Satisfied FRE 502(b)(3) Obligation, http://www.ediscoverylaw.com/2011/09/articles/case-summaries/court-denies-motion-to-exclude-inadvertently-produced-email-rejects-argument-that-26b5b-request-for-the-emails-return-satisfied-fre-502b3-obligation/print.html, *last visited* June 28, 2012.

[15] Pacific Coast Steel v. Leany, No. 2:09-cv-12190, 2011 WL 4573243, 2011 U.S. Dist. LEXIS 113849 (D. Nev. Sept. 30, 2011).

[16] *Id.* at *7–8, *11, 2011 U.S. Dist. LEXIS 113849, at *24.

fidentiality of E-Mail Communications with One's Client, addresses the danger of third-party access to client communications.[17] The opinion discusses two common examples of how the attorney-client privilege can be put at risk: employer-provided email, where the employer has indicated that it has the right to monitor emails (and the party communicates with counsel via the email account), and where a family member can access an email account (and the party is involved in a matrimonial dispute). The opinion, which echoes a number of recent cases, suggests the need to educate the client about this risk and obtain consent of how he/she would like to be communicated with.

A quick search of the K&L Gates database[18] of electronic discovery cases related to email in 2012 illuminates a number of common themes, including spoliation and sanctions;[19] privilege and waiver;[20] forensic examination of email accounts;[21] cost shifting for processing email accounts,[22] and motions for a protective order over email records, emails, text messages, and other related information from Yahoo and Verizon.[23]

There have been predictions that use of email would by now be passé and would be bypassed in favor of texting, tweeting, and social media, at least within popular culture. However, from these cases it is clear that email continues to be a major means of communication within the business community, so it still should be a matter of concern in the context of electronic discovery, as well as for overall information management.

2.   *Possession/Custody/Control*

[Add the following text at the end of the section.]

In 2012, the American Bar Association Commission on Ethics 20/20 has circulated drafts of amendments to rules and comments that reflect the modern realities of the practice of law, particularly issues that relate to the increasing use of technology to manage law firms and to deliver

---

[17]ABA Standing Comm. on Ethics & Prof'l Responsibility, Formal Opinion 11-459, Duty to Protect the Confidentiality of E-Mail Communications with One's Client (Aug. 4, 2011), *available at* http://learn.uvm.edu/ce/wp-content/uploads/ABA_Formal_Opinion.pdf (last visited June 28, 2012).

[18] E-Discovery Case Database, K&L Gates, http://www.ediscoverylaw.com/articles/ediscovery-case-database/, last visited September 11, 2012.

[19]Danny Lynn Elec. v. Veolia Es Solid Waste, No. 2:09CV192, 2012 WL 786843, 2012 U.S. Dist. LEXIS 31685 (M.D. Ala. Mar. 9, 2012); Hudson v. AIH Receivable Mgmt. Servs., No. 10-2287, 2012 WL 1194329, 2012 U.S. Dist. LEXIS 49189 (D. Kan. Mar. 14, 2012).

[20]Goldstein v. Colborne Acquisition Co., No. 10 C 6861, 2012 WL 1969369, 2012 U.S. Dist. LEXIS 75743 (N.D. Ill. June 1, 2012); Jacob v. Duane Reade, Inc., No. 11 Civ. 0160, 2012 WL 651536, 2012 U.S. Dist. LEXIS 25689 (S.D.N.Y. Feb. 28, 2012).

[21]Moore v. Kingsbrook Jewish Med. Ctr., Nos. 11-CV-3552, 11-CV-3624, 2012 WL 1078000, 2012 U.S. Dist. LEXIS 45738 (E.D.N.Y. Mar. 30, 2012).

[22]Rawal v. United Air Lines Inc., No. 07 C 5561, 2012 WL 581146, 2012 U.S. Dist. LEXIS 21880 (N.D. Ill. Feb. 22, 2012).

[23]Special Mkts. Ins. Consultants, Inc. v. Lynch, No. 11 C 9181, 2012 WL 1565348, 2012 U.S. Dist. LEXIS 61088 (N.D. Ill. May 2, 2012).

legal services more efficiently and economically. A number of materials were filed with the ABA House of Delegates on May 7, 2012, for consideration at the ABA's annual meeting in Chicago in August 2012. Among the filings were resolutions and reports on technology and confidentiality, technology and client development, and outsourcing that could encompass email and other electronic means of communication within law firms, with clients, and with third parties and which may depend on the services of third-party and Cloud computing vendors.[24]

On August 6, 2012, the ABA's House of Delegates voted to approve changes to the ABA Model Rules of Professional Conduct "to provide guidance regarding lawyers' use of technology and confidentiality as follows ...."[25] Resolution 105A makes several changes regarding email:

- Model Rule 1.0 Terminology: In Section (n), "e-mail" is amended to "electronic communications";

- Model Rule 1.0, Comment [9] (Screened): Screening includes avoiding contact with or denying access to "information, including information in electronic form," which relates to the matter;

- Model Rule 1.1 Competence, Comment [6] (Maintaining Competence): Rule 1.1's admonition that a lawyer should maintain "requisite knowledge and skill" by keeping "abreast of changes in the law and its practice" now includes in such practice "the benefits and risks associated with relevant technology";

- Model Rule 1.6 Confidentiality of Information: Section (c) is added whereby "A lawyer shall make reasonable efforts to prevent the inadvertent or unauthorized disclosure of, or unauthorized access to, information relating to the representation of a client." The expectations are illuminated in the amendments to Comment [16] (Acting Competently to Preserve Confidentiality);

- Model Rule 4.4 Respect for Rights of Third Persons: Section (b) now adds "electronically stored information" as material whose inadvertent receipt requires a prompt notification to the sender;

- Model Rule 4.4, Comment [2] describes how a document or electronically stored information is inadvertently sent when it is accidently transmitted, for example, as when an email or letter is misaddressed.[26]

---

[24] See ABA Commission on Ethics 20/20, available at http://www.americanbar. org/groups/professional_responsibility/aba_commission_on_ethics_20_20.html (last visited June 28, 2012).

[25] Resolution 105A Revised, http://www.americanbar.org/content/dam/aba/ administrative/ethics_2020/20120808_revised_resolution_105a_as_amended. authcheckdam.pdf. http://www.americanbar.org/content/dam/aba/administrative/ ethics_2020/20120808_revised_resolution_105a_as_amended.authcheckdam.pdf (last visited September 11, 2012).

[26] Id.

Lawyers are urged to review these proposed revisions to the Rules as well as to read the report that accompanies these revisions to fully understand what their ethical responsibilities may be, given that many if not most states are likely to adopt the same or similar revisions. In addition, lawyers will want to review the revisions in Resolution 105B dealing with technology and client development to see the extent to which it impacts advertising and solicitation using email or other electronic means as well as the multijurisdictional practice of law.[27]

C. Cross-Border Issues

[Add the following text at the end of the section.]

Outsourcing of many of the functions of a law firm may raise cross-border issues with respect to email and other electronic communications. As part of its work, the ABA Commission on Ethics 20/20 recently released its resolution and report dealing with outsourcing.[28] Among the revisions approved by the ABA House of Delegates in August 2012 are the following changes:

- Model Rule 1.1 Competence, Comments [6] & [7] (Retaining or Contracting With Other Lawyers): These two new Comments illuminate the ethical responsibilities for retaining or contracting with other lawyers. One aspect of this that is related to cross-border issues is the possibility that these lawyers may be located in other countries, thus necessitating the need to communicate via email and other electronic means which may not necessarily be protected by laws and regulations in those counties, as well as making sure that lawyers in those countries are properly apprised of their responsibilities for handling confidential materials in a secure manner. (Former Comment [6] is redesignated as Comment [8] (Maintaining Competence).)

- Model Rule 5.3 Responsibilities Regarding Nonlawyer Assistance: In the title, a subtle but significant change is made from "Assistants" to "Assistance." New Comments [3] & [4] address the use of nonlawyers outside the firm and provide as examples the hiring of a document management company to create and maintain a database for complex litigation, sending client documents to a third party for printing or scanning, and using an Internet-based service to store client information. Comment [3] makes it clear the lawyer must make reasonable efforts to make sure that services

[27]Resolution 105B, *available at* http://www.americanbar.org/content/dam/aba/administrative/ethics_2020/2012_hod_annual_meeting_105b.authcheckdam.pdf (last visited June 28, 2012).

[28]Resolution 105C, *available at* http://www.americanbar.org/content/dam/aba/administrative/ethics_2020/2012_hod_annual_meeting_105c.authcheckdam.pdf (last visited June 28, 2012).

that are outsourced to nonlawyers are provided in a manner that is compatible with the lawyer's professional obligations. This Comment also references several of the other rules, including Rule 1.1 Competence, Rule 1.6 Confidentiality, and Rule 5.5(a) Authorized Practice Of Law.

III. Issues Arising Out of Impermissible Use of Email

A. Spam

2. *The CAN-SPAM Act*

a. *What Is Covered*

iii. "Hybrid" Messages

[93][In footnote 93, correct the *MySpace* WL citation to "2007 WL 1686966."]

v. "Initiating Transmission"

[Add the following text at the end of the section.]

The question of what constitutes "initiat[ing] the transmission" of covered emails arose recently in the context of social media messaging in *Facebook, Inc. v. Power Ventures, Inc.*[29] Defendant Power Ventures, Inc. offered users the ability to access multiple social networking accounts through a single, integrated Web site at www.power.com. As a promotion of its Web site, Power offered users the chance to win $100 if they successfully invited and signed up new Power.com users. Power used participants' Facebook login credentials to obtain a list of their Facebook friends, and asked the participants to select which of those friends should receive an invitation to a Facebook "event" promoting Power's Web site. Those invitations purported to come from "Facebook" and used an "@facebookmail.com" address, not a Power.com address.[30]

In cross-motions for summary judgment, the parties disputed whether Power "initiated" the emails at issue or whether, as Power argued, Power could not have initiated the emails because the emails were authorized by Facebook users and sent from Facebook's own servers. It was undisputed that:

---

[29]No. C 08-05780, 2012 WL 542586, 2012 U.S. Dist. LEXIS 25062 (N.D. Cal. Feb. 16, 2012).

[30]*Id.* at *1, 2012 U.S. Dist. LEXIS 25062, at *5.

(1) Power.com authored the text contained in the emails and provided the link contained therein that would allow recipients to sign up for Power.com;

(2) the launch promotion feature that offered the $100 reward was made available through Power.com (not through any social network);

(3) Power created and used a script that would automatically send event invitations to a user's Facebook friends;

(4) Power paid 30 to 40 people who got 100 or more friends to sign up, and

(5) Power.com's "offer of potential monetary compensation may have induced some Facebook users to participate in Power's launch program."[31]

The court found Power "originated" the emails by intentionally causing Facebook's servers to send emails written by Power, through the use of a software program Power specifically created to cause Facebook's servers to send those emails.[32] To the extent that Facebook users authorized any of these actions, the court found that Power procured that authorization by "offering and awarding monetary incentives."[33]

---

[31] *Id.* at *6, 2012 U.S. Dist. LEXIS 25062, at *20–21.
[32] *Id.* at *7, 2012 U.S. Dist. LEXIS 25062, at *22.
[33] *Id.*, 2012 U.S. Dist. LEXIS 25062, at *22–23.

14

The Law of Virtual Property

Michael J. Meehan, JD, PhD.

Patent Counsel
Mountain View, California

165

I. Introduction

[Add the following text after the carry-over paragraph on page 751.]

In January 2012, the Dutch Supreme Court decided a case on the theft of virtual property in the game RuneScape, which is a popular multi-user online game in which players can obtain virtual goods, including armor and weapons. Once the player has found or "earned" a virtual good, the bits associated with the virtual good are associated with the player's account.[1] In the case heard by the Court, a 13-year old boy was coerced by two older boys into going to one of their houses. While there, the defendants told the boy to transfer a virtual amulet and mask from his RuneScape account to one of theirs. When the victim refused to transfer his virtual goods, they beat him until he complied.

The primary issue the court had to resolve was whether the virtual property qualified as a "good" under Article 310 of the Dutch Penal Code, and therefore whether the act could be considered theft.[2] The Court's analysis paralleled the concepts laid out by Meehan in 2006. That paper states that keys to attributing real-world value to virtual property in multi-user virtual societies and games are non-replicability and persistence of the virtual property. The paper also states that the protection should be afforded to the bits in the context of the game.[3] The court looked to the value subjectively attributed by both the victim and the attackers, to suggest that the virtual property had fair market value, notwithstanding that

[1]RuneScape, Beginner's Guide, What's Next?, *available at* http://www.runescape.com/beginnersGuide_whats_next.ws (last visited April 28, 2011).

[2]HR 31 January 2012, LJN BQ9251, NJ 2012, §2.3, *available at* http://zoeken.rechtspraak.nl/detailpage.aspx?ljn=BQ9251 (last visited August 29, 2012). A rough, unofficial English translation is available at http://static.ow.ly/docs/LJN%20translation_uem.pdf.

[3]Michael Meehan, *Virtual Property: Protecting Bits in Context*, 13 Rich. J.L. & Tech. 7 (2006), *available at* jolt.richmond.edu/v13i2/article7.pdf.

no numeric value was attributed to the virtual property in this case. The value is attributable to the ability to use the virtual amulet and mask in the context of the game. Both the victim and the assailant stated that having control over the virtual amulet and mask make the virtual property owner *rijk* ("rich") within the context of the game.[4]

The court looked to the fact that the stolen goods were not a replica of the original goods, but were instead first under exclusive control of the victim and later under the control of the assailant. Stated another way, the bits of data associated with the virtual goods were first associated with the account of the victim and, after the theft, associated with the account of one of the assailants. This transfer of non-replicable data from one account to another, providing exclusive control to the assailants, was the act at issue in the theft.[5]

In responding to pleadings by the defense, the court dismissed the notion that, although Jagex Ltd. oversaw the control of the virtual property associated with the accounts via its operation of the game, that ownership could not be imparted to game players. The Court also stated that although the virtual goods may fall under the definition of "data" under other sections of the Dutch Code, it can also be a "good" under Article 310. The Court went on to state that the virtual property was not *louter illusive* (roughly, "mere illusion") for which aspects of ownership and theft are not possible.[6]

II. WHAT IS VIRTUAL PROPERTY?

A. Conceptualizing Virtual Property

4. *Protection Should Be for the Particular Integer (Bits) as Used in the Game (Context)*

[18][In footnote 18, correct the *Bragg v. Linden Research, Inc.* citation reporter to "F. Supp. 2d".]

III. SUMMARY OF THE *LINDEN RESEARCH* VIRTUAL PROPERTY CASES

B. *Evans v. Linden Research, Inc.*

[58][In footnote 58, update the *Evans v. Linden Research, Inc.* citation to "763 F. Supp. 2d 735, 741 n.6 (E.D. Pa. 2011)".]

---

[4]LJN BQ9251, *supra note* 2 at §2.3.
[5]*Id.* at §§2.2–2.3, 3.5, 3.6.1.
[6]*Id.* at §2.3.

Table of Cases

*References are to chapter and footnote number (e.g., **4:** 24, 29 refers to footnotes 24 and 29 in Supplement Chapter 4). MV indicates an update in this supplement to a footnote in the main volume (e.g., **MV8:** 218 refers to footnote 218 in Main Volume Chapter 8). For the updates to the main volume, only new cases are included in the table.*

O

Omega S.A. v. Costco Wholesale Corp., 541 F.3d 982, 88 USPQ2d 1102 (9th Cir. 2008) *4:* 11<n>13

Oracle Am., Inc. v. Google, Inc., No. 10-03561, 2012 WL 1964523, 2012 U.S. Dist. LEXIS 75896, 103 USPQ2d 1023 (N.D. Cal. May 31, 2012) *4:* 1, 2, 5, 7; *6:* 40<n>51

Original Creations, Inc. v. Ready Am., Inc., 836 F. Supp. 2d 711 (N.D. Ill. 2011) *12:* 20<n>24

P

Pacific Century Int'l, Ltd. v. Does 1-37, No. 12 Civ. 1057, 2012 WL 1072312, 2012 U.S. Dist. LEXIS 44368, 102 USPQ2d 1201 (N.D. Ill. Mar. 30, 2012) *5:* 66

Pacific Coast Steel v. Leany, No. 2:09-cv-12190, 2011 U.S. Dist. LEXIS 113849, 2011 WL 4573243 (D. Nev. Sept. 30, 2011) *13:* 15, 16

Patrick Collins, Inc.
—v. Does 1-18, No. 2:11-cv-07252, 2012 WL 1686071 (E.D. Pa. Mar. 8, 2012) *4:* 36<n>38
—v. Does 1-2,590, 2011 WL 4407112 (E.D. Pa. 2012) *4:* 23

Perfect 10, Inc.
—v. Amazon.com, Inc., 508 F.3d 1146, 99 USPQ2d 1746 (9th Cir. 2007) *6:* 23, 25
—v. Cybernet Ventures, Inc., 213 F. Supp. 2d 1146 (C.D. Cal. 2002) *6:* 87
—v. Visa Int'l Serv. Ass'n, 494 F.3d 788, 83 USPQ2d 1144 (9th Cir. 2007) *7:* 83

Perfumebay.com, Inc. v. eBay, Inc., 506 F.3d 1165, 84 USPQ2d 1865 (9th Cir. 2007) *1:* 2

Personal Keepsakes, Inc. v. PersonalizationMall.com, Inc., No. 11 Civ. 5177, 2012 WL 414803, 2012 U.S. Dist. LEXIS 15280, 101 USPQ2d 1855 (N.D. Ill. Feb. 8, 2012) *5:* 20<n>28

PETA v. Doughney, 263 F.3d 359, 60 USPQ2d 1109 (4th Cir. 2001) *7:* 24

Petroliam Nasional Berhad v. GoDaddy.com, Inc., No. C 09-5939, 2012 U.S. Dist. LEXIS 156, 101 USPQ2d 1507 (N.D. Cal. Jan. 3, 2012) *8:* 1<n>5

Pollstar v. Gigmania Ltd., 170 F. Supp. 2d 974 (E.D. Cal. 2000) *9:* 18

Q

Quality King Distribs., Inc. v. L'Anza Research Int'l, Inc., 523 U.S. 135, 45 USPQ2d 1961 (1998) *4:* 8<n>10

R

Rawal v. United Air Lines, Inc., No. 07 C 5561, 2012 WL 581146, 2012 U.S. Dist. LEXIS 21880 (N.D. Ill. Feb. 22, 2012) *13:* 22

Reed Elsevier, Inc. v. Muchnick, 130 S. Ct. 1237, 176 L. Ed. 2d 18, 93 USPQ2d 1719 (2010) *4:* 18, 19

Roger Cleveland Golf Co. v. Prince, No. 2:09-CV-2119, 2010 WL 5019260, 2010 U.S. Dist. LEXIS 128044 (D.S.C. Dec. 3, 2010), *motion denied,* No. 2:09-CV-2119, 2012 WL 1106775, 2012 U.S. Dist. LEXIS 46065 (D.S.C. Mar. 30, 2012) *7:* 56, 64<n>72

Rosetta Stone, Ltd. v. Google, Inc., 730 F. Supp. 2d 531, 97 USPQ2d 1855 (E.D. Va. 2010), *aff'd in part, vacated in part, remanded,* 676 F.3d 144, 102 USPQ2d 1473 (4th Cir. 2012) *1:* 5<n>26; *7:* 15, 16, 20<n>27, 29<n>40, 42<n>51, 74<n>86; *MV7:* 121, 529, 890, 900

S

Sands, Taylor & Wood Co. v. Quaker Oats Co., 978 F.2d 947, 24 USPQ2d 1001 (7th Cir. 1992) *7:* 50

Sara Lee Corp. v. Kayser-Roth Corp., 81 F.3d 455, 38 USPQ2d 1449 (4th Cir. 1996) *1:* 12